Pornography

Debating the Issues

Ted Gottfried

—Issues in Focus—

Enslow Publishers, Inc.

44 Fadem Road   PO Box 38
Box 699   Aldershot
Springfield, NJ 07081   Hants GU12 6BP
USA   UK

For Harriet:
Peace and Love

Library of Congress Cataloging-in-Publication Data

Gottfried, Ted.
    Pornography : debating the issues / Ted Gottfried.
        p. cm. — (Issues in focus)
    Includes bibliographical references and index.
    Summary: Provides a history of pornography in the United States and
discusses the pros and cons of the issue.
    ISBN 0-89490-907-X
    1. Pornography—United States—History—Juvenile Literature.
    2. Pornography—Moral and ethical aspects—United States—Juvenile
literature. [1. Pornography.] I. Title. II. Series: Issues in focus (Hillside,
N.J.)
    HQ472.U6G67   1997
    363.4'7'0973—dc20   96-34291
                                                          CIP
                                                          AC
Printed in the United States of America

10 9 8 7 6 5 4 3 2 1

Cover Illustration: Enslow Publishers, Inc.

Contents

Acknowledgments

I am grateful to Bob Peters of Morality in Media and Kate Lang of the National Coalition Against Censorship for their help in assembling material for this book. As always, I am also indebted to those at the Mid-Manhattan branches of the New York Public Library, as well as the Central Research Library, the Epiphany Branch of the Public Library, and the central branch of the Queensboro Public Library. Thanks are also due to my friend Janet Bode, and—with much love—my wife, Harriet Gottfried, who—as always—read and critiqued each chapter of this book as it was written.

All contributed, but any shortcomings in the work are mine alone.

1

What Is Pornography?

What people call pornography can be a book or a magazine, a story or a poem. It can be a painting, a sculpture, or a photograph. It can be a movie or a play, a TV show or a live show. Pornography can be watched, listened to, read, or even touched.

But what is it? What *is* pornography? *Webster's* dictionary says pornography is "writings, pictures, etc. *intended* to arouse sexual desire."[1] In other words, pornography is something that excites you on purpose. But sex alone is not pornography. When something is pornographic, says *Webster's*, it is "obscene,"[2] which means it is "offensive to modesty or decency; lewd; impure," and even "foul, filthy, repulsive" and "disgusting."[3]

Offensive to Decency

The problem is that what is disgusting to some people is not at all disgusting to others. For instance, a few years back there was a campaign to put clothing on dogs, cats, and other pets to cover their nudity. Some people were offended by the sight of these animals' sex organs. They were obscene to them. The majority of people, however, were not bothered at all. So far, the majority has prevailed. The law may require Fido and Lassie to be leashed, or muzzled, but they can still run around naked.

People cannot. They may take advantage of beaches or camps set aside for nudists, but there are laws against their going without clothes in the towns and cities of America. While there may be exceptions, there is general agreement that public nudity is—as *Webster's* defines obscenity—"offensive to decency."[4]

Eye of the Beholder

This would seem to fall under the heading of "family values." Americans do not want their children exposed to the sight of naked people in public places. Yet in Japan, where family values are generally much more strongly in place than in the United States, whole families—mother, father, children of both sexes—go naked in public baths along with other families who are equally naked. On the other hand, most Japanese are shocked by the widespread availability in America of what they consider "pornography."

What is acceptable in one place is not acceptable in another. What is pornographic to one person is art, or perhaps just entertainment, to another. To some extent then, pornography is a matter of where it is encountered and who is doing the encountering. The first step in deciding what is pornography is taken by individuals deciding for themselves.

But who will decide for society as a whole? Is it really necessary that this be done? Are some things so offensive to so many people that society must act to protect itself from them? Does pornography have an effect that goes beyond offending, an influence that provokes deeds that everyone agrees are evil and perhaps criminal? Does it cross the line into action, and if so, should it be banned before the damage can be done?

Many people, for an assortment of reasons, and to varying degrees, believe that society has a right to protect itself in this way. Reflecting their concern, lawmakers— city, county, state, and federal—fashion laws that they believe will reasonably restrict pornography. The problem is that such laws almost always use the words "pornography" and/or "obscenity" to define that which should be restricted. Those who enforce the laws, and those who sit in judgment on people accused of breaking them, must bring their own understanding of what the words mean to their roles.

Knowing It When You See It

One who faced this problem was future justice of the U.S. Supreme Court Potter Stewart. In 1964, he sat in a lower court and was the sole judge of a French film, *The Lovers,* which the government was attempting to have banned as hard-core pornography. ("Hard-core"—in today's terms—means that it was frank and blatant, in your face, as opposed to soft-core, which either hinted and implied, or tantalized and teased, depending on who was describing it.)

Federal Judge Stewart decided that the film should not be banned as obscenity. Many were displeased by this decision, and some were outraged. When he was confronted, Judge Stewart admitted that he could not define obscenity. But, he added, "I know it when I see it."[5]

Those who were against any form of censorship used Potter's words to prove how vague definitions of pornography were. If even a judge whose job it was to decide what was and what was not pornography could not define it, they said, then surely it was hopeless to try. And if it could not be defined, then how could it be censored? How could it be banned?

But such arguments have not solved the problem of what to do about the effects of pornography. Isn't some pornography so bad, so extreme that the only purpose it serves is evil? Consider works where violence is a key part of the sex being portrayed. What about kiddy porn in which underage children engage in sex acts, sometimes with adults? Or snuff movies, in which a real person is allegedly killed in order to arouse the viewer?

Whose Eye? Which Beholder?

Pornography, like beauty, may be in the eye of the beholder, but surely not all beholders are equal. Should the opinions of the clergy and the sex offender be given equal weight? If children are at risk, isn't giving up the right to watch X-rated videos in the privacy of one's own home a small price to pay to keep them safe?

Perhaps *Lolita*, the novel by Vladimir Nabokov about a man obsessed with little girls, is a work of art, but if it encourages sick men to take advantage of innocent children, then would society not be better off without it? This is the point on which opinions divide. People who might outlaw kiddy porn are not happy with the idea of banning a literary novel. They point to similar themes involving children in Greek mythology, sacred Asian writings, Shakespeare's plays, even the Bible.

If you ban artistic works like *Lolita*, where do you stop? they ask. To which the other side replies that if you ban nothing—if anything is permitted—where will the harm to society stop?

Is there a middle ground between these two views where reasonable regulations might be applied without becoming oppressive? If so, then exactly where is that middle ground? And how do we get people to agree on it?

Hopefully, the following chapters will help you to consider—if not answer—these questions.

2

Smut or Art?
A Historic Question

From earliest times, in many different cultures, the arts and literature have been concerned with subjects that are taboo to some people. Stone Age drawings of human stick figures engaging in sex acts found on the walls of caves in France may date back as far as forty thousand years. Representations of erotic activity discovered in the Ur excavations of Mesopotamia were produced around 3000 B.C. In China, during the Han Dynasty (206 B.C.–A.D. 220), "spring coins"[1] depicting acts of love were given to children "as a form of protection against supernatural forces."[2] Between the sixth and seventeenth centuries A.D., the Hindu temples of India were decorated with graphic sex scenes by unknown sculptors. Mayan vases found in Peru were fashioned to resemble men's sex organs.

The ancient Greeks turned out pottery, coins, sculptures, and tapestries that left nothing to the imagination.

Like similar items from ancient Japan, these exaggerated both size and activity. Indeed, "sex was worshipped as sacred in the Mediterranean regions,"[3] as it was in other early cultures around the world.

There were also early efforts to suppress such works. In 213 B.C., hand-written, decorated pornographic scrolls were forbidden by the Chinese emperor Shih Huang-ti. Those who failed to destroy them were punished with branding by hot irons and forced labor. In ancient Greece (470 B.C.), one of the crimes for which Socrates, a Greek philosopher, was put to death was "corrupting the morals of the young"[4] with his teachings in the public squares of Athens. However, in early times most of the population lived outside of the cities. Provocative speech, works of art, and writing had limited circulation. It wasn't until the invention of the printing press in the fifteenth century that taboo materials could be mass produced and distributed in quantities that threatened the morals of the larger society.

Revising the Bible and Shakespeare

Reproduced by printing presses, the Bible and the works of Shakespeare were for many years the most widely distributed literature. In the early nineteenth century, English language versions of both were rewritten to remove offensive language. By then the effect of circulating lewd writings and pictures had become of concern to pious people everywhere. In 1802, in England, the Society for the Suppression of Vice was established to ban works that might arouse the passions of the impressionable poor.

Dr. Thomas Bowdler was a member of the society. In 1818, he came out with *The Family Shakespeare*, from which all the "blemishes" included "to please a licentious age"[5] had been removed. Although there were objections from scholars to the altering and removal of portions of Shakespeare's writing, the fact is that today it is Bowdler's version of the plays that most people read, or see performed. Now, when a work is censored and offensive language removed from it, we say that it has been "bowdlerized."

In 1833, the American Noah Webster, famous for his dictionary, bowdlerized the Bible. His reasoning was that "many words and phrases are so offensive, especially to females, as to create a reluctance in young persons to attend Bible classes and schools in which they are required to read passages which cannot be repeated without a blush."[6] He took out whole verses because they were "beyond the reach of effective bowdlerization,"[7] and changed many words to make them more acceptable.

Both Bowdler and Webster claimed to have noble motives. They did not censor for the sake of censoring. Bowdler truly loved Shakespeare's plays and believed that by taking out the language that offended they would be read by more people. Webster was concerned that biblical language was offensive to the religious people of a later and more civilized time and that it would keep them from reading the Good Book.

The Obscene Publications Bill

Preserving the works of Shakespeare and the Bible may have been the goal of bowdlerization, but the trend regarding less worthy works viewed as obscene was definitely toward banning them altogether. In England, the Obscene Publications Bill was passed in 1857. It said that booksellers and librarians could be jailed for offering banned books. The British philosophers Herbert Spencer and John Stuart Mill both opposed the measure on the grounds that it interfered with freedom of expression. Its main effect, however, was to persuade publishers to censor themselves and not publish works that might cause them to be prosecuted.

One who did not do that was Henry Vizetelly, the English publisher of the novel *La Terre*, by the renowned French author Emile Zola. In 1888, Vizetelly was arrested and brought to trial for "publishing obscene literature."[8] When he was convicted and sent to prison, *The Methodist Times* proclaimed that "no one can read Zola without moral contamination."[9]

Zola had set the style for the literary movement that would come to be known as naturalism. His realistic style portrayed people as sexual beings with earthy desires. He, and the writers inspired by him, focused on the seamier side of life. Zola himself wrote novels dealing with passion, murder, drunkenness, and prostitution. The people in his novels were often the dregs of society who did not observe the niceties of those with more money and higher social status.

Those who wanted to ban the works of naturalist writers were motivated by a concern that people should strive to be better than they are, not wallow in their animal natures. Often they were religious people who resented the portrayal of humans as beasts, rather than as

14

God's creatures living moral lives. Key to their objection was the belief that words affected behavior, that by portraying immorality the naturalists were encouraging it. They saw such writing—and some still do—as a threat to civilization itself.

This was—and is—as true in the United States as elsewhere. In the nineteenth century, works by Benjamin Franklin, Mark Twain, and Ambrose Bierce were all banned as pornographic. Nor was American censorship limited to writings or always exercised nonviolently.

The Big Bad Bull

In 1871, the Bull's Head Tavern and Gambling Saloon was opened in the frontier town of Abilene, Kansas. It was owned and run by a much-feared gunslinger named Ben Thompson and his partner, Phil Coe, a gambler from Texas. They had a giant bull painted across the front of the building housing the saloon. It was described as "a bull of monumental proportions with certain anatomical features [the bull's sex organs] enlarged even beyond the enormous scale of the rest of the painting."[10]

Word of the painting spread and cowboys and gunslingers came to Abilene to see it for themselves and to have a drink, or a round of poker, at the Bull's Head Tavern. Some of them behaved pretty wildly, which did not make the law-abiding citizens of the town too happy. Also, the decent, churchgoing folk were embarrassed by the bull and concerned about its effect on their children. They asked their town marshal to do something about getting rid of it.

His name was Hickock—Wild Bill Hickock—a lawman known for his skill as a gunfighter throughout the West. He gave the owners of the saloon twenty-four hours to remove the obscene bull. When they did not do so, Wild Bill took matters into his own hands. He came back with a can of black paint and a brush and painted over the most offensive part of the bull's anatomy.

Phil Coe was furious. He went gunning for Hickock. In the ensuing gunfight, Wild Bill killed him. Ben Thompson—wisely—sold the saloon and left town. The bull came down.

Back East, two years later, the New York Society for the Suppression of Vice was started. It crusaded for decency less lethally than Wild Bill Hickock had, but it was just as effective. During its first ten years, between 1873 and the end of 1882, the society was "responsible for 700 arrests,"[11] for "the seizure of 27,856 pounds of obscene books,"[12] and for destroying 64,836 of those "articles for immoral use"[13] that we call condoms. But that was nothing to the record racked up by its secretary, Anthony Comstock, during his long career as a smut-buster.

"Comstockery" in Action

Anthony Comstock was born in New Canaan, Connecticut, in 1844. When he was eighteen years old, Comstock broke into a local liquor store and let the beer out of all of the barrels. Then he went off to fight for the Union in the Civil War (1861–1865). After the war he went to New York City where he became active with the Young Men's Christian Association (YMCA). He campaigned with the YMCA to lobby Congress to pass a law forbidding transportation of obscene materials through the mail. In 1873, the same year that the New York Society for the Suppression of Vice was formed, the federal law was passed. It became known as the Comstock Act.

Acting under the Comstock Act, the U.S. Post Office Department appointed Comstock as special agent authorized to enforce the new law. From 1873 through 1906 he served without pay. Altogether, he served for forty-two years, until his death in 1915.

During that time, Comstock claimed to have destroyed "sixteen tons of vampire literature"[14] and to have convicted for obscenity "enough persons to fill a passenger train of sixty-one coaches."[15] *Leaves of Grass* by Walt Whitman, a leading poet in America at that time, was banned because of Comstock. He was also responsible for banning the books of birth control crusader Margaret Sanger, as well as for closing some of her clinics.

When Comstock prevented performances of *Mrs. Warren's Profession*, by George Bernard Shaw, the world-renowned Irish-British playwright's revenge was to coin the word "comstockery," which is still used as a synonym for overzealous and prudish censorship. Shaw himself defined comstockery as "the world's standing joke at the expense of the U.S." because it "confirms the deep-seated conviction of the Old World that America is a provincial place, a second-rate country town."[16] As if to prove Shaw right, Comstock's campaign to force publishers to rid their books of "explicit language"[17] resulted in the substitution of the French word "*enciente*" for the

English word "pregnant"[18]—probably on the theory that nobody would understand it in translation.

September Morn

Comstock's most famous case involved prints of an oil painting by Paul Chabas entitled *Matinee Septembre*. The picture—*September Morn,* as it was called in the United States—showed a nude young woman turned sideways and wading in a pond. The pose had been "rejected as being too tame for a barber shop calendar,"[19] but a New York art dealer had bought two thousand prints, intending to sell them retail.

The dealer hired a publicist named Harry Reichenbach to promote sales of the prints. Reichenbach put one of the prints in the window of the store and called Comstock. Pretending to be an outraged minister, he told him that there was a disgusting nude on display in a store window on Fourth Avenue "and little boys are gathering around there to look at her."[20] He then gave a group of boys a quarter each to stand in front of the window with their mouths open. Comstock arrived and ordered the dealer to "remove that filthy picture." When the dealer refused, Comstock had him arrested.

But the court that tried the dealer on obscenity charges found him not guilty. The judge said the picture was innocent and no threat to the boys' morality. Thanks to the wide publicity generated, over 7 million copies of *September Morn* were eventually sold while jokes and songs poking fun at Comstock were heard on vaudeville stages all across the country.

Nevertheless, in 1915, shortly before Comstock's death, President Woodrow Wilson named him United States representative to the International Purity Congress held in San Francisco, California. While he was there, Comstock arrested some department store window dressers for allowing their wax models to appear naked where passersby could see them. The case was dismissed with the judge telling him, "Mr. Comstock, I think you're nuts."[21]

It is easy to poke fun at Comstock today. But it must be remembered that he lived in a time when most Americans were very concerned with maintaining conservative standards. Women dressed modestly in long dresses that concealed even their ankles. Sex was not a matter to be openly discussed. Family values were not a political slogan, but a fact of life for most Americans even as they either ignored or deplored the exceptions.

Making fun of Comstock was not necessarily fair. He deeply believed he was fighting the good fight against the devil's work. Most clergy members of most religions agreed with his efforts most of the time. When he died, *The New York Times* praised his "courage and energy . . . [in] the protecting of society from a detestable and dangerous group of enemies."[22] Comstock waged a powerful crusade with strong support in an age of innocence, but times were changing.

In the years following Comstock's death, just before and after 1920, the new theories of Sigmund Freud on the causes of human behavior began to take hold in America. Sex played a large part in them. Many Americans were offended by this, but others felt liberated.

They were the ones who ushered in the so-called Flapper Era of the 1920s, marked by illegal drinking of liquor, cigarette smoking in public by women as well as by men, uninhibited dances like the Charleston and the Black Bottom, skirts worn above the knees, and necking in the backs of cars. The challenge to America's entrenched morality was profound.

The War on "Dirty Books"

For whatever reason, this challenge was met by an attack on books—mostly novels—that were believed to encourage the flamboyant behavior of young people. It was as if, unable to control the children, Americans decided to declare war on dirty books. In a way they were saying what had been said by guardians of decency since Gutenberg invented the printing press: Morality begins with the word.

An early target was James Joyce's erotic novel *Ulysses*, which the *Encyclopaedia Brittanica* calls "a masterpiece of world literature."[23] *Ulysses* was written in Zurich, Switzerland, between 1915 and 1920. Portions of it began to appear in short installments in a Paris magazine in 1918. That same year, episodes were reprinted in *The Little Review*, a New York magazine.

On October 4, 1920, the publishers of *The Little Review* were arrested on obscenity charges. They were subsequently convicted on the grounds that *Ulysses* was "capable of corrupting a young girl."[24] However, while there is little doubt that *Ulysses* was more frank and con- tained more graphic sex scenes than anything being

20

published in the United States at that time, its fate was not sealed by that first trial.

What the trial did do, though, was have a chilling effect on the publication of other novels containing erotic material, or language thought to be offensive. Throughout the 1920s, works by Thomas Mann, Virginia Woolf, D. H. Lawrence, and Radclyffe Hall—among many others—were banned in the United States. Other works were revised by the editors, or by the authors themselves, to get around the obscenity laws.

This had already happened to Theodore Dreiser as early as 1900, when he had been forced to agree to the removal of words and scenes from his novel *Sister Carrie*—now an American classic. (It would be the 1990s before his original version of the book was published.) By the 1920s, Dreiser had become America's leading realist writer. Then, in 1925, he wrote *An American Tragedy*, which critics acclaimed as "the greatest American novel of our generation,"[25] but which was banned in Massachusetts as an obscene book. There was a trial, which Dreiser and his publishers lost, followed by an appeal to the state supreme court, which they also lost.

The Supreme Judicial Court of Massachusetts said that "nothing essential . . . would be lost" if passages that were "indecent, obscene and manifestly tending to corrupt the morals of youth" were taken out. The court went on to express its fear that "the obnoxious passages" might be read by children who "would continue to read on until the evil effects of the obscene passages were weakened or dissipated . . ." The effect on children of a work written for adults was an argument that had been

21

heard many times before and would be heard many times again.

The case against *An American Tragedy* was brought because after the book was banned, one of its publishers arranged to be arrested for selling a copy. The laws against obscenity—not just in Massachusetts, but in most states as well as in England and France—held that booksellers, printers, and publishers were as guilty when it came to breaking the obscenity laws as those who created the offending work. This resulted in many writings not being published, printed, or distributed because of fear of going to jail.

While many books of literary merit, such as *Lady Chatterley's Lover*, *Tropic of Cancer*, *The Well of Loneliness*, *God's Little Acre*, *Strange Fruit*, and *The Memoirs of Hecate County*, continued to be banned throughout the next few decades, there were also smutty books of no literary merit whatsoever that were written, printed, and published with an eye toward having them banned. The idea was to have them banned in one place—Boston, say—and then to cash in on the publicity through sales in other communities before they could get around to banning them.

The *Ulysses* Standard

The practice raised interesting questions: Was obscenity acceptable if a book conformed to some high literary standard? If that was so, who decided the standard, and what was it? And was it fair to restrict reading to those who had been educated up to the standard? Wasn't that just what they had tried to do in England in 1802 when

22

they banned works that might arouse the passions of the impressionable poor? Was pornography acceptable for the elite, but not for others?

In a way these questions were addressed in the next trial involving *Ulysses*. In 1932, an edition of the book had been seized by customs agents on the grounds that obscene material could not be imported into the country. Random House, which wanted to actually publish the book in the United States, hired lawyers to challenge the decision to ban it. The case was heard by Judge John M. Woolsey in federal court.

In Judge Woolsey's opinion, the "correct" standard for obscenity was to decide if a book "tended to stir the sex impulse or to lead to impure and lustful thoughts."[26] But Judge Woolsey was quite clear that in the eyes of the law there were to be no differences among readers. His standard applied to "the man on the street," the person "with average sex instincts."[27] He concluded that *Ulysses* did not arouse. When the case was appealed by the government, the U.S. Court of Appeals upheld him and *Ulysses* was at last published in the United States.

Ulysses may be a masterpiece, but it is a dense work and not easy to read. Those concerned with protecting public morals were not really too concerned about its availability. Other, more readable works, however, continued to be banned. As the years went by, where obscenity was concerned, the printed word was well under control in the United States. But then came the 1960s, and the focus shifted to the spoken word and a nightclub comedian named Lenny Bruce.

23

Foul Language

Lenny Bruce was arrested for the first time at the Jazz Workshop in San Francisco, California, in October 1961. The charge was obscenity. Bruce had spoken a forbidden word aloud.

He had spoken it in a nightclub to a selective audience who had paid to hear him say it. There were not supposed to be any minors in the audience, nor was it suggested that there were any, and if any of the paying customers were offended, they did not say so. One observer, however, was offended. He was a police officer and he arrested Bruce. It was only the first of many such arrests of Lenny Bruce for using dirty words in nightclubs around the country.

It should be made clear that forbidden words were a deliberate part of Bruce's act. He said that he used them as a matter of principle. It is also true that they pulled people into the clubs he worked. But he was sincere in his belief that words were just words—means of communication—and that there was no such thing as bad words and good words.

Many of the words he used described bodily functions and sex acts. He felt that suppressing them was the same as lying. "If you *do* them," he insisted, "you should be able to *say* the words."[28]

Bruce is long dead, but the words he used are spoken pretty openly today in films, and sometimes on television. Sometimes the acts to which they relate are shown too. But should they be? Is it okay to view them because the words are now used so openly? Or are the people who want to restrict the language correct? Do words lead to actions, and do fictional portrayals of actions provoke actions in real life? Is the breakdown of society feared by Bowdler and Comstock and their successors actually happening today?

What do you think?

Magazines, Movies, and TV: From Cheesecake to Prime Time

Those who believe pornography is harmful regard the obscene word, whether written or spoken, as a power for harm or evil. But obscenity that is actually seen, rather than merely described, may be much more powerful. Language provides fantasy, but to see pornography is to immediately experience the effect—perhaps the shock— of its graphic message. The impact is visual and direct.

When Anthony Comstock looked at the print of *September Morn* in the window of that art store, he saw obscenity. Others merely saw a not-too-revealing nude. Some thought the picture was artistic, and some did not. Others were aroused by it to varying degrees; this proved to some that the picture was obscene; but others did not object to being aroused.

Calendars and Nudes

In 1913, an illustrated calendar was brought out featuring *September Morn*. It was not the first so-called pinup calendar featuring images of immodestly clad women in provocative poses. The first had appeared in 1904, starting a trend that continued through World War II, when pinups of movie stars like Betty Grable and Lana Turner in bathing suits, or tight sweaters, were popular with servicemen. But *September Morn* was the first completely nude calendar illustration. It became famous, but not as famous as the Marilyn Monroe calendar released almost forty years later with nude photographs of the film star.

The Monroe calendar was released in the 1950s. Her naked poses shocked and offended some people. They missed the artistic elements that Tom Kelly had tried to capture. He had decided to photograph Monroe because "there was a natural grace about her." It was feared that the calendar might put an end to her film career just as it was beginning. That did not happen—perhaps because so many filmgoers saw what Kelly had seen.

Portrayals of naked human bodies have always been looked at as both obscene and artistic. The Spanish artist Francisco Goya, whose career continued from the eighteenth into the nineteenth century, had it both ways. He did two paintings of the beautiful Duchess of Alba, one as *The Dressed Maja*, and one as *The Nude Maja*. Goya regarded the body as "a disguise for the soul."[1] His question—should the soul be hidden, or revealed?—is the question art asks about the human body. One answer was given by Pennsylvania State University officials in 1992 when a reproduction of *The Nude Maja* was removed from a classroom wall because of a professor's complaint that "it made her and her female students 'uncomfortable.'"[2]

Both male and female nudes have always been popular subjects for artists. At the beginning of the Edo Period (1600–1868) in Japan, naked figures were the opening wedge of "a quite unparalleled development of erotic art and literature."[3] The period ended when "the Japanese government started to take an interest in censorship."[4] The pattern has been repeated many times in many cultures around the world. Nudity may be the first sign of danger to those concerned about pornography.

French Postcards and Flip Books

The first French postcards—so-called because they were manufactured in Paris and sold to tourists from other countries—were produced around 1900. They showed women in bathing costumes, but were soon followed by cards displaying nudes. These were followed by French postcards featuring a variety of erotic poses. The earliest featured drawings and paintings, but later there were photographs of real naked people—men and women—performing all-too-real acts. It was not long before these postcards were being sold in countries all over the world.

Pornography is never far behind technology. In the early 1900s, the stereoscope was developed. This was a hand-held viewer designed to create a three-dimensional effect. Nudes were one of the first subjects of the pictures sold for stereoscopes. More graphic pornography soon followed.

Technology, however, was already moving beyond still photographs. Movies were already being shown in theaters. Curiously enough, the principle behind them—that of moving photographs swiftly in order to create motion—was adapted in a much simpler and cruder form to create a type of pornography that would prove to have particular appeal to children. This would outrage people who would not, perhaps, be moved to action by pornography for adults.

Flip books, as they were called, consisted of pages of drawings—sometimes merely stick figures—arranged in sequence. When the pages were flipped, the figures would seem to move and there would be the illusion of action.

Flip books were cheap to manufacture. The most basic story line was of a person undressing. As the pages were flipped, the clothes came off until the person was nude. Other sequences were more involved—and more obscene.

There were several reasons why they appealed to children. They were cheap to buy, selling for as little as a penny in the early days, only a nickel or dime forty years later, and perhaps as little as fifty cents even today. They were small, usually no larger than a cigarette pack, and easy to hide. They were usually cartoony, and those who liked comic books liked that. They could be viewed privately, and innocent children could learn about various sex acts for the first time without being embarrassed. Young people who would have had no idea how or where to acquire adult porn introduced each other to flip books.

Those who produced them were not slow to realize who their market was. The knowledge focused their distribution efforts. Long before drugs and guns were a threat to the schoolyard, flip book pornography had established a market there.

The flip books were—and are—viewed by many as an assault on the innocence of children. Antipornography crusaders pointed out that they distort and cheapen sex by turning acts of love into the unreal action of comic strips. Such distortions, they feared, can affect the children's sex lives later on. The children must be protected, they insisted. A line must be drawn between freedom of expression and the duty to safeguard the young.

Stag Movies

Through the years, there have been many laws against material like flip books in the cities and towns of the United States. They have, for the most part, not worked. Nor did such laws have much effect on the underground smut movies that were already being made and distributed illegally at the same time that production of legitimate silent films for theaters was beginning.

Because it was cheaper, the early smut films were mostly made abroad and smuggled into the United States. They were known as stag movies because they were mostly purchased by men's clubs, fraternities, or other men's groups to be viewed without women present. The women in the films were being presented for the male viewers' entertainment, but the women in their lives were barred from seeing them.

31

The legitimate movies of the early silent era, while not comparable to the stag movies, or even to the frank films of today, were quite daring compared to those that would follow when Hollywood established self-censorship. There were occasional glimpses of forbidden body parts in epics such as the 1915 film *Intolerance*. The love scenes—for that age—were quite torrid. Both adultery and premarital sex were common themes. Altogether, the values of the Hollywood films as the 1920s began were a far cry from those of most of their audiences. There were frequent protests about the films even as attendance at movie theaters rose.

Of more concern, however, was the behavior of the stars. When the suicide of Olive Thomas, whom Selznick Pictures had billed as the "Ideal American Girl,"[5] was followed by the headline "OLIVE THOMAS DOPE FIEND,"[6] Cardinal Mundelein of Chicago wrote and distributed a pamphlet called "The Danger of Hollywood: A Warning to Young Girls."[7] It had little effect. A year later, an up-and-coming starlet named Virginia Rappe died during rough sex allegedly forced on her by one of the screen's top comedians, Fatty Arbuckle. After two hung juries, Arbuckle was tried again and acquitted, but Paramount canceled his $3 million contract and his career was ended.

Around this time, top director Desmond Taylor was murdered. During the investigation that followed, it came out that "he had been carrying on simultaneous affairs with Mabel Normand, Mary Miles Minter and Charlotte Shelby, Mary's mother."[8] Both Minter and

Normand were popular movie stars. The scandal ruined the careers of both.

The Motion Picture Production Code

The real-life Hollywood scandals and what was considered racy and vulgar material on the screen merged in the public mind and the protests mounted. To deal with it, in 1921, the United States Motion Picture Producers and Distributors of America hired Will H. Hays, a former postmaster general of the United States who had enforced the Comstock Law. One of his first acts was to insert a "morality clause"[9] into all actors' contracts. This meant that if they were involved in scandals in their private lives, the studios could fire them immediately.

However, the Hays Office—as it came to be known—"was an organization with little clout during the 1920s, created merely as a smokescreen to keep the federal government from imposing its own brand of censorship or control over the wild and woolly film business."[10] That changed in the early 1930s, soon after sound was added to film, because of "Mae West's suggestive humor, Jean Harlow's sexiness, and a rash of violent gangster films."[11] The movies of Mae West in particular struck some filmgoers as an assault on decency. In one, she replied to a question about her many love affairs by defining what really counted: "It's not the men in my life, but the life in my men,"[12] she purred, turning 1930s morality on its head.

Such dialogue would be considered tame today. So too would the loosely clothed sexiness of Jean Harlow and the violence of films like *Public Enemy* and *Little Caesar*. Nevertheless, in 1930, the industry adopted a Production Code that the Hays Office began enforcing in earnest in 1934. The code imposed a time limit on movie kisses, outlawed any profanity stronger than "drat," did not allow words like virgin, pregnant, and syphilis to be spoken, prohibited even married characters from sharing the same bed, banned all nudity—even of infants—frowned on cleavage, and insisted that sin had to be punished. Happy endings were encouraged. Leading film critic George Jean Nathan said that the effect of the code was to present screen lovers as "little children dressed up in their parents' clothes and playing house."[13]

The power of the code was that no movie could be released for distribution without a seal of approval. This could be strictly enforced because the movie studios owned the theater chains where the films were shown. In 1950, however, an antitrust action by the federal government declared this illegal and the theaters had to be sold.

Producers could now make their own deals with theaters without the studios' okay. When Otto Preminger's film *The Moon Is Blue* was denied a seal of approval because it "dealt explicitly with the issue of virginity,"[14] he released it anyway. The code-breaking publicity made it a hit at the box office and soon other producers were following suit. By the 1960s, the Production Code was no longer an effective tool in censoring movies.

What followed in films was pretty much what the antipornographers had feared and predicted. There was a flood of films dealing with forbidden themes, using forbidden language, and displaying nudity. In 1967, the film *Bonnie and Clyde* ushered in an era of movie violence that continues to the present day. The combination of sex and violence in movies has been blamed for provoking a rise in sex crimes in the United States.

X-rated Cassettes

In the 1960s, underground sex films began surfacing. They were being produced in the United States now, rather than abroad. The quality got better, the films were less grainy and in color, and dialogue and simple plots were added to the nudity and sex scenes. Theaters devoted to showing both male/female and same-sex pornography sprang up in the larger cities around the country. At first they did not advertise, but word spread among those who wanted to view such material and attendance mounted. Soon theaters devoted to such films were operating openly in sleazy entertainment areas that also offered live shows featuring nudity and sex acts.

With the advent of VCRs, X-rated cassettes featuring every conceivable sort of sexual activity have become available for rental. Sometimes used as sex aids, they are watched by women as well as by men. The stag films of yesteryear are no longer stag. Today, X-rated films are a major part of the billion-dollar pornography business.

Pornographic Magazines

Once the core of that business was magazines. The first English language pornographic magazine appeared in Great Britain in 1773. It was called *The Covent Garden Magazine*. It was followed ten years later by *The*

Rambler's Magazine, which was devoted to tales of women "whom the attracting charms of gold can conquer"[15]—meaning that they sold sexual favors. But these publications were not illustrated.

The most famous pornographic magazine of the Victorian Era, *The Pearl*, appeared in England in 1879. It too was composed mostly of text, but during its seven years of publication it did offer "36 obscene colored lithographs" of "vile execution."[16] *The Pearl* was circulated underground, as were similar magazines that came out in both England and the United States.

It was not until the 1930s that the first "girlie magazines"[17] were sold openly in the United States. They "were intended to be *respectable*, emphatically not 'pornographic.'"[18] *Esquire* led the way with "pin-ups."[19] Drawn by George Petty, they looked more like cartoon figures than real women. There were protests from groups concerned with morals, but sales were good and the Petty Girl was soon appearing regularly in the magazine. In 1941, *Esquire* introduced a centerspread foldout featuring the Petty Girl.

In 1953, *Playboy* magazine appeared to challenge *Esquire* with a combination of flippant text and revealing photographs intended for a young male bachelor audience. At first the pictures were not even seminude. Rather they were artful poses of well-endowed young women in bathing suits that seemed too small for them. After a while these young women began to appear topless, but carefully positioned so that the upper parts of their bodies were not clearly visible.

Playboy was immediately and immensely successful. Many imitators—*Dude, Gent, Scamp, Bachelor,* and others—sprang up. So too did another kind of magazine that took its lead from *Playboy,* but imitated only one aspect of it. These were magazines like *Follies, Frolic,* and *Gala,* which consisted of nothing but pictures of scantily clad women identified by captions, or short blocks of text. They were called cheesecake magazines and they made no pretense of appealing to anything but men's interest in women's bodies.

Post Office Rules

The publishers had to be very careful in doing this. More than forty years after the death of Anthony Comstock, the Post Office still enforced strict rules regarding what kind of materials could be transported through the United States mail. Also, magazines were shipped bulk mail at a lower rate, and publishers were in danger from issue to issue of having that privilege taken away from them. Without it, most could not have afforded to publish.

As a result of this, both the cheesecake magazines and *Playboy* and its imitators had to be very careful in the way they presented photographs. The Post Office was constantly changing the rules, or reinterpreting them. This led to bizarre retouching of the pictures in order to cover over, or even remove, various parts of the bodies in the photographs. Editors and art directors would crouch over light boxes with magnifying glasses arguing over what the Post Office might or might not consider a forbidden hair.

These magazines were constantly under attack from antipornography groups. Yet the pictures in them showed nothing like what can be seen on the movie screen today. Indeed, the most harmful result of the early cheesecake magazines may well have been the distorted pictures of women's bodies that some young men carried around in their heads after looking at the retouched pictures.

Over the following decades, however, while the cheesecake magazines pretty much faded away, the Post Office taboos were relaxed. *Playboy* imitators, and then *Playboy* itself, moved from seminude to nude pictures, to focusing on sex organs and finally on erotic activity. This sort of thing reached its peak in the 1970s with *Hustler* magazine and its presentation of what many consider sadistic and disgusting acts.

By then the sexual revolution was in full swing. It seemed that nothing was forbidden to say, to write, to look at, or to actually do. That permissiveness continued. Pictures that were forbidden in the cheesecake magazines of the 1950s are now found every Sunday in the magazine sections of respectable newspapers like *The New York Times.*

Even pornographic comic books are sold openly today. That is very different from the situation in the 1950s, when quite ordinary comic books came under attack for drawings of women clothed in futuristic costumes and for presenting action scenes thought to be too violent. In 1954, psychiatrist Dr. Frederic Wertham, author of the best-selling book *Seduction of the Innocent,* led a movement claiming that children were adversely affected by the comics. This led to Senate hearings on the connection between comic books and juvenile crime. The furor died down when the comic book industry agreed to regulate itself. Actually, the 1950s comic book costumes were no more provocative than the clothes worn today, and the POW!-BAM! violence was tame compared to that seen on prime-time television.

Sex and Violence on TV

Looking at today's TV, it is hard to believe that when programming started at the end of the 1940s television defined itself with show after show stressing family values. Today, instead of the wholesome values of *Leave It to Beaver, Father Knows Best,* and *The Brady Bunch,* regular network TV offers prime-time sex and violence via such shows as *Melrose Place, NYPD Blue, Beverly Hills 90210,* and *Law & Order.* Afternoon programming is filled with steamy soap operas and with frank talk shows covering once forbidden topics in uncensored depth. Real-life stories of brutality and lust are recreated as dramatized specials. (There were three dramatizations of the Amy Fisher-Joey Buttafuoco case involving statutory rape and attempted murder.) And there is a constant parade of such exploitative shows as *Hard Copy* and *Inside Edition.*

Cable TV goes even further with such programs as *Reel Sex* on Time Warner's HBO channel. On other channels, X-rated movie porn stars have emceed programs on lovemaking techniques. Nudity and sex acts have been shown. In some parts of the country there are channels set aside for sexy programming.

Antiporn Leaders: Speaking Out

On standard TV, even the nightly news is covered with an emphasis on sex and violence. The trial of pro-football star O. J. Simpson for murder repelled many viewers. Russell Shaw, director of public information for the Knights of Columbus, observed that "the Simpson coverage has been the media equivalent of a giant peep show—a huge exercise in pandering to prurient curiosity."[20]

The sex-and-violence content of TV has brought calls for action from religious leaders and antipornography groups. A 1994 World Communications Day statement by Pope John Paul II advised that "forming children's viewing habits will sometimes mean simply turning off the television set."[21] In February 1995, this prompted the antipornography organization Morality in Media to sponsor a "Turn Off TV Day" to protest graphic programming. Finally, on January 8, 1996, the U.S. Supreme Court upheld a lower court ruling that because society has a "compelling interest in protecting children,"[22] such programming could be broadcast only during "late-night hours when children are less likely to tune in."[23]

Many news organizations, civil liberties groups, and individuals in the arts protest the Supreme Court decision. They see it as an opening wedge to further censorship and control of TV. Peggy Charren, head of Action for Children's Television, argues that "too often we try to protect children by doing in free speech. Indecency to some people might be sex education, and that's the problem. Who defines indecency? The censors define it."[24]

So it is that the age-old questions are raised again in connection with television: What effect does objection-able material *really* have on children? On family values? On the stability of society? How much control over media is justified? And how much constitutes a threat to our basic rights as Americans?

4

The Case for
Banning Pornography

*Pornography is to freedom of expression what anarchy is
to liberty; as free men willingly restrain a measure of
their freedom to prevent anarchy, so must we draw the
line against pornography to protect freedom of expression.
Moreover, if an attitude of permissiveness were to be
adopted regarding pornography, this would contribute to
an atmosphere condoning anarchy in every other field—
and would increase the threat to our social order as well
as to our moral principles.*[1]

—President Richard M. Nixon

In the decades since President Nixon defined the scope of
the issue, writes Archbishop John P. Foley of the
Pontifical Council for Social Communications, "the
offensive, exploitative treatment of sex and violence by
the media . . . has become a serious worldwide
problem."[2] The reason, according to a report by the

43

council, is that "at a time of widespread and unfortunate confusion about moral norms, the communications media have made pornography and violence accessible to a vastly expanded audience, including young people, and even children."[3] According to the antipornography organization Morality in Media, this has had a variety of harmful effects. Among them is pornography's role in inspiring crimes of sex and violence.

Studies by the Federal Bureau of Investigation's behavioral science unit reveal that "about 80 percent of killers who commit sexual crimes have a taste for violent pornography."[4] A workshop conducted by the U.S. Surgeon General's Office has concluded that "exposure to violent pornography increases punitive behavior towards women."[5] And the United States Attorney General's Commission has found that "nonviolent pornography whets the appetite for violent forms."[6]

Jerry R. Kirk, president of the National Coalition for the Protection of Children & Families, is more specific. "*Playboy* and *Penthouse*," he believes, "are the marijuana that leads to the crack and cocaine of hard-core and child pornography."[7] One of the last statements by serial killer Ted Bundy indicates just how far that path can lead someone.

Pornography and Sex Crime

Bundy, who raped and murdered an unknown number of victims, was executed in 1989 for killing a twelve-year-old girl. Shortly before his death, Bundy discussed his addiction to pornography with a psychologist. "I would keep looking for more potent,

44

more explicit, more graphic kinds of materials," Bundy said, adding that finally "you reach the jumping-off point where you begin to wonder if maybe actually doing it will give you that which is beyond reading about it or looking at it."[8]

Once that point is reached, it is hard to tell where behavior that is experimental crosses over into behavior that is unnatural, or where behavior that is unnatural becomes behavior that is criminal—and sometimes deadly. In the so-called Preppy Murder Case a few years back, rough sex between nineteen-year-old Jennifer Levin and Robert Chambers led to her death and his conviction for first-degree manslaughter. The type of behavior that led to that tragedy is glorified graphically and in detail in the Japanese film *In The Realm of the Senses*, which was widely distributed in major cities throughout the United States.

The movie was a reenactment of an actual sex crime committed in Japan. However, sex-and-violence scenes in films are not always reenactments. In snuff films available on videocassettes, real people were allegedly killed during rough sex.

Whether such deaths are reality or illusion, the porn films in which they occur can be a learning experience. In his 1992 report *Pornography's Effects*, Dr. Victor B. Cline points out that "at the very least, pornography educates."[9] A government consultant and psychotherapist who specializes in sexual addictions, Dr. Cline agrees with those religious leaders and parents who believe that porn should not be used in sex education for children.

Soft-core and Hard-core

Their objections begin with soft-core porn. This would include magazines, books, or films that feature gutter language, show nudity, or present scenes of conventional lovemaking meant to arouse the viewer or reader. By their standards, magazines like *Playboy*, books like *Lady Chatterley's Lover*, and films like *Waiting to Exhale* fall into the category of soft-core porn.

Hard-core porn is judged even more objectionable by antipornography activists. The term refers to material showing or describing acts that deviate from normal sex, conduct that is disgusting, or depraved, involves perversion, bathroom functions, or violence. *Hustler* magazine, Bret Easton Ellis's novel *American Psycho*, and the movie *Basic Instinct* are regarded as hard-core by many.

Such material, they believe, reduces the person to the lowest animal level. In their view, the human body is a temple and sex is a God-given function. This function involves love and marriage and having babies so that humanity will go on; it is not merely an amusement to pass the time like going to a ball game, or a movie.

A basic objection to pornography is that it presents sex as divorced from love, and even affection. Confirmation of this comes from an unexpected source. In Denmark, where pornography is legal, a young girl reacted to what she found at a Porno-Fair with these words: "There is complete lack of every kind of affection and solicitude for the other partner," she reported.[10]

That is a major point for those who want to stop the flow of obscene materials. They believe that pornography turns sex from something beautiful into something dirty.

And when it does this, there is a ripple effect as in throwing a stone into a pond.

Family Values

The stone first strikes at the very heart of family values. It presents behavior that is immoral and sinful as acceptable. Pornography makes premarital sex and adultery and a variety of other perversions not only permissible, but attractive. It encourages both male and female homosexuality—lifestyles that are not acceptable to many people.

Nor is it only those who come into direct contact with pornography who are affected. The ripples spread, and with them the effects of smut on the community as a whole. The Pontifical Council's report cited strong evidence that obscene materials "corrode human relationships, exploit individuals—especially women and young people, undermine marriage and family life, foster anti-social behavior and weaken the moral fiber of society itself."[11]

Even nonviolent pornography is harmful according to a study by Dr. Dolf Zillman and Dr. Jennings Bryant. After weeks of exposure to soft-core material, those who participated in the experiment said they felt "less satisfaction with their partner's sexual performance, affection and physical appearance." After assessing the results of Zillman and Bryant's study, sex addiction expert Dr. Cline concluded that "this would suggest that the consumption of pornography erodes marital values and the institution of marriage itself."[12] This may be borne out

by escalating divorce rates over the years in which
pornography has flourished.

The Price of Smut

Organizations like Morality in Media and the Knights of
Columbus believe that soft-core pornography also
encourages premarital sex, and so must share the blame
for the results. Their view is that increasing sexual
activity among young people today can be directly traced
to their constant exposure to the pornographic content
of the books and magazines they read and the movies and
television programs they watch. In addition to the
content, the message of permissiveness—that sex is cool
for young people and everybody's doing it—is a powerful
one playing into the need for peer approval. They
wonder how many young people have sex only because
they do not want to be labeled square, or be rejected, or
feel left out.

An article in the 1994 book *Teenage Sexuality* is a
reminder that "teenage pregnancy in the U.S. is the highest in the world—over one million each year with more
than half ending in abortion."[13] Material that encourages
premarital sex bears a strong responsibility for the rising
rate of out-of-wedlock births in our country. Many of
these young, single mothers end up on welfare. Both
mother and child are trapped in a situation of depen-
dency. Apart from the harm done to the individuals
involved, the burden on local, state, and federal govern-
ments is increasing at an alarming rate.

The number of unmarried young women and ado-
lescents who become pregnant and resort to abortion is

even more distressing to some antipornography crusaders who regard abortion as baby killing. It should be noted, however, that not everybody who is against porn agrees with this position. There is wider agreement that much premarital sex is the result of an ongoing permissiveness encouraged by the media.

Back in 1989, outraged antiporn fighters organized a campaign against Madonna's sexy music videos, provocative statements, and steamy picture book *Madonna's Sex*, which featured scenes of rape and bestiality. As a result, Pepsico canceled a television commercial featuring the pop singer. In the aftermath, there was a decrease of sexual behavior in shows on prime-time TV. However, in 1993, *Journalism Quarterly* found that "sex is being used in promotion commercials for prime time programs at a rate 16 times higher than the sexual activity in the programs themselves."[14] More recently, there has been a call to put more effort into "national campaigns against sponsors of obscene and offensive [and popular] TV programs."[15]

Grass-Roots Action

Leaders of the campaign against pornography also urge grass-roots action on the local level. This means organizing against the X-rated video rental stores, adult movie houses and peep shows, topless and nudie bars, and newsstands plastered with obscene magazine covers that corrupt many city neighborhoods. A child who passes these places on the way to and from school every day is being introduced to sex in its most vulgar and distorted forms. How can that not have a destructive effect on the child's own developing sexuality? Porn

49

fighters ask, if one is presented daily with sex as violence, how can one not grow up believing that sex and violence are one?

There is a meeting ground here between those who believe sex education should be taught in the schools and those who do not. The point of agreement is that "sex is already being taught to youngsters through the wide distribution of pornography."[16] Henry Boatwright, chairperson of the U.S. Advisory Board for Social Concerns, reports that "70 percent of all pornographic magazines end up in the hands of minors."[17] Antiporn crusaders view that as reason enough to drive those magazine stands that peddle them out of residential neighborhoods, and areas near public and parochial schools.

Some pornography, however, is not just in the neighborhood; it is in the home. Recently, more and more children are being introduced to porn on their household telephones. Dial-A-Porn is a multimillion dollar dirty-talk business by which calls may be made to numbers offering discussions of every kind of sexual perversion. Ads in many magazines and newspapers give the numbers to call. Usually, ads note that the caller must be eighteen or older to use the service. The cost can run as high as three dollars or more a minute. (It should be noted that Dial-A-Porn is also a source of vast profits to various telephone companies.) Some of the calls involve party lines with two or more panting voices describing the sickest kinds of sex acts to the child. Conference calls offering group sex fantasies are also available. Some children have run up thousands of dollars in billing on their parents' phones before they were stopped.

Young Sex Offenders

Dr. Victor Cline conducted a pilot study for the U.S. Department of Justice on the effects of Dial-A-Porn. He found that "in every case, without exception, the children [girls as well as boys] became hooked on this sex by phone and kept going back for more and still more." He thought the conclusion was inescapable: Dial-A-Porn had an "addiction effect."[18] Police statistics indicate that an increasing number of young people addicted to hard-core pornography are acting out what they have learned. Recent cases include sexual assault on a two-year-old girl by two Detroit boys (one was only eleven years old), the rape of a mentally retarded girl by five New Jersey teenagers using a broomstick and a miniature baseball bat, and a gang of boys age twelve to seventeen raping and brutally beating a woman jogger in New York City's Central Park.

"Nationally," reports *The New York Daily News*, "the number of reported incidents [of children committing sex crimes] has been increasing for a decade."[19] Mental health professionals estimate that young girls commit between 10 percent and 20 percent of reported sex crimes. Richard Weiss, who runs a Wayne County, Michigan, program that has treated over one hundred adolescent sex offenders, says that "there's not a kid in our program who has not been involved with pornography."[20]

Many of these young abusers have themselves been abused. Sometimes this has occurred when they are very small, only three or four years old. Sometimes the one who abused them is a family member, sometimes a baby-sitter, or a friend of the family. Pornography commonly plays a part in the abuse, either in terms of arousing the molester, attracting the child's interest, or showing the child what to do. Former Los Angeles Police Chief Daryl F. Gates and Detective Ralph W. Bennett of the Sexually Exploited Child Unit of the Los Angeles Police Department point out that "the frequent recovery of pornography in sexually exploited child cases is not considered to be happenstance."[21] It is a part of the pattern.

The Youngest Victims

The children most exploited by pornography, of course, are those who appear in it. Throughout the 1970s, child pornography could be purchased openly from adult bookstores and skin-magazine vendors. This was the period during which a major studio released a feature film called *Pretty Baby*, which portrayed Brooke Shields as a child prostitute living in a brothel, as well as offering nudity and sex scenes. It was not covered by the federal Protection of Children Against Sexual Exploitation Act passed in 1977.

Of course the exploitation of Brooke Shields was not comparable to that of the children who appear in child pornography. She was only acting; they are actually performing the obscene acts shown. Outrage at children being misused in this way has led twenty-two states to make the possession of child pornography a criminal offense.

What about the other twenty-eight states? There is opposition in them from those who believe that all pornography is an expression of free speech. Antiporn crusaders answer them by pointing out that children, some of them lured, some of them kidnapped, have been trapped or forced into committing the most revolting acts. Some of these children are as young as five or six years old. Is not the person who buys the pornography in which children appear as much a part of the crimes committed against them as the kidnapper, the child molester, and the photographer, or moviemaker, who profits from the terrible things done to these innocents? This is not, the foes of pornography insist, what the framers of the Constitution meant by free speech!

How to Fight Back

The most frequent charge leveled against those who fight what they regard as filth is that they are in favor of censorship. They deny this. "The term censorship," according to Morality in Media, "involves prior restraint of First Amendment rights by government."[22] They are not asking for this. All they are asking for is that federal and state laws against pornography be strongly enforced.

"The U.S. Supreme Court," they say, "has repeatedly held that obscenity is NOT a First Amendment right."[23] What is a constitutional right is the right of citizens to demonstrate against stores peddling pornography. There is also a right to protest violence and vulgarity on TV, and to organize not to buy the products of the sponsors responsible for its being there. And—most importantly—there is a right to try to vote into office those people who will champion the cause of ridding our society of the pornography—and of voting out of office those who shirk that responsibility.

53

Antipornography activists claim that they are not for censorship; they are for decency. Young people of today may not remember when decency was the rule, but it really was not that long ago. It was a time when you could turn on your TV set and find dialogue without profanity, affection without perversion, and performers who kept their clothes on.

Wasn't that a wonderful time?

5

The Case Against Censorship

Well no, it was not such a wonderful time according to those who view antipornography campaigns as a threat to their rights and liberties. Actually, they say, it was a head-in-the-sand time when the human body was regarded as shameful, when sex was a taboo topic, when suppression of natural impulses was the rule and frustration the frequent condition. It was a time when ignorance and guilt limited the lovemaking of passive women and clumsy men. It was a time when babies' hands were tied down to keep them from touching their private parts, when information about birth control could not be distributed, when the only safe place for gay people was in the closet. It was an unreal time.

Reality is key to those who oppose the smut-busters. They look at the world around them and conclude that erotic materials must be fulfilling a need. Although nobody can say exactly how large the sex industry is in the United States, it is expanding so rapidly that the most conservative estimates put the annual gross at well over $10 billion. That reflects a major market. Call it pornography, or call it erotica as those who champion it do, there is no denying that it has the very widest popular appeal.

Whether the product is nudity and straightforward sex or sex and violence, soft-core or hard-core, straight or gay, there are buyers for it in the United States. They include men and women of all ages from every ethnic and racial group. They also include, frequently in contrast to the official position of their religion, people of every denomination.

Within this market there are frequent shifts. Magazine sales, while still in the millions monthly, are on the decline. Publication of erotic paperbacks has also fallen off. Network television, reacting to pressure, is cutting back on the sex-and-violence content of its prime-time programming.

On the other hand, Dial-A-Porn continues to grow as do audiences for cable TV sex shows and pornography on the Internet. The X-rated sections in video stores account for 25 percent of rentals, with some store owners reporting that women are renting them in increasing numbers. It is the technology that has changed, not the public appetite for sexually explicit material.

An industry this large creates jobs and stimulates the economy. It pays substantial taxes. It requires no help from the government in the form of subsidies as—for instance—the tobacco industry does. And it satisfies a basic law of supply and demand—a demand, its defenders point out, that if not satisfied legally will undoubtedly be met illegally.

Repression and Rape

Industry spokespersons do not agree with the charges of indecency and immorality made by the antipornography movement. They question the alleged harmful effects of sexually explicit material on society and its children. They point out that critics' attitudes toward so-called pornography are determined by their attitudes toward sex itself.

They believe that many of their opponents take their lead from antiporn crusaders like Bishop Donald Wuerl, who has written of sex as the "original sin and its results the human condition,"[1] by which he means the state of sin in which all people live because of the role that sex played in creating them. This kind of thinking, industry spokespeople say, confirms attitudes toward sex that are narrow and restrictive, old-fashioned and out-of-touch with the society in which we live. It leads to conclusions that have no basis in fact, they say, such as that there is a cause-and-effect relationship between sexually explicit materials and sex crime.

Publisher of *Screw* magazine Al Goldstein not only takes issue with the idea of cause and effect, he claims that the opposite is true. He says that when the sex urge is repressed, it may explode in acts of rape and violence against women. He believes we should be looking for ways to make pornography better, rather than banning it.

There are psychiatrists and psychologists who agree with what Goldstein is saying. They see sex criminals as individuals who routinely repress their sex urges. This suppression builds the pressure that explodes into antisocial acts. Pornography offers them a substitute release.

Evidence to back this up came from Denmark in the 1970s. During the first twelve years following changes in Danish law that made distribution of erotic materials legal, there was "a dramatic decrease in reported sex crimes."[2] This inspires such people as Edward De Grazia, the author and lawyer who successfully fought to free Henry Miller's book *Tropic of Cancer* from censorship, to recommend the "decriminalization of obscenity and pornography"[3] as a way of getting rid of the "criminal porn-manufacturing industry"[4] responsible for snuff films and child pornography.

The Right to Enjoy Erotica

As for crimes of rape and child abuse and serial murder, blaming the erotica industry for them outrages those in the business. A publisher of adult magazines who has produced X-rated films and appeared in them herself points out:

> The volume of sexually explicit material out there indicates that most of the people in this country must be reading skin magazines, or looking at erotic video cassettes, or reading sexually explicit books. However, ninety-nine-point-nine percent of them are not raping, or murdering, or abusing children. Even assuming that those who commit such acts do so because of their use of pornography—which I don't for a minute believe because the motivations in such cases are just not that simple and clear-cut—but assuming it anyway, does that mean that the vast

majority who do not act out should be denied access to the material? By that logic, nobody should ever have a cocktail because of the small percentage of drinkers who turn into drunk drivers and kill pedestrians. How far do you go with that kind of reasoning? How much of people's freedom do you take away? Where does it end?[5]

Others echo her concern. They point out that putting restrictions on people's use of erotica is often only the first step in taking away other rights. When Libyan dictator Muammar al-Qaddafi seized power, one of his first acts was to close down the shows featuring belly dancers in revealing costumes that were a hallmark of the nightclubs in the capital city of Tripoli. He personally led a platoon of soldiers into a night spot called the Bowdlerina, marched up onto the stage where sixteen dancers were performing, pulled his revolver from his holster, and fired three shots into the ceiling. As the terrified female dancers dived for cover, he announced that "this evil place is officially closed as of now."[6] To make sure it would not reopen, his soldiers chopped it down with axes.

Within days, Qaddafi had shut down every enterprise having to do with sex in Tripoli. Even as his antisex campaign spread throughout the rest of Libya, he began restricting the freedom of newspapers and radio stations, taking over businesses to be run by the state, and passing law after law limiting the freedom of private citizens. Qaddafi is not the only example of this. Journalist Pete Hamill, writing in *Playboy*, points out that "the sexual restrictions of Stalin's Soviet Union, Hitler's Germany and Mao's China would have gladdened the hearts of those Americans who fear sexual images and literature." Hamill added this chilling warning: "Every tyrant knows that if he can control human sexuality, he can control life."[7]

The excuse for controlling erotica, point out those who oppose such control, goes back to the idea that sex itself is sinful. Not all cultures, by any means, have this view. There have been many societies that have viewed sex joyously, rather than fearfully, with an eye toward pleasure, rather than guilt. There have been nations like Denmark that have recognized that erotica relieves society of the notion that sex is sinful. In such places pornography widens the scope of what society views as normal, and therefore helps in ending discrimination against homosexuals, lesbians, and others who are too often viewed as unnatural.

Also, the case is made that erotic materials contribute to the raising of sexual consciousness that some view as necessary to the liberation of women. Pornography and women will be discussed in detail in the chapter that follows, but it should be noted here that those who believe pornography is liberating believe that if it has done nothing else, it has introduced women to the idea that they are as entitled to take pleasure in sex as men are. In past years in this country, this notion was not a common one.

Explicit Fantasy Therapy

The liberating effects of erotica have been noted by many marriage counselors, psychiatrists, and psychologists. It can be a marital aid, relieving inhibitions, or suggesting ways to improve the husband-wife relationship. Such

60

material can be particularly useful in marriages where there are sexual problems.

"As a board-certified clinical sexologist," wrote Patti Britton, Ph.D., to a 1992 Senate Judiciary Committee considering pornography legislation, "I can tell you that it is common knowledge in my field that sexually explicit films and videos are often recommended as a mode of treatment for couples or individuals with clinical sexual problems. Such materials are viewed by professionals as helpful, not harmful, assets in the treatment process."[8]

Spokespersons for erotica point out that sex is a mental and emotional process as well as a physical one. The extent of mental and emotional involvement is directly related to the depth of pleasure experienced. Fantasy plays a large part in this. "Pornography," the renowned psychoanalyst Otto Kernberg told a Columbia University seminar, "can stimulate an active fantasy life—can be an antidote to stifled passion."[9]

Indeed, many counselors use such materials as a means of rekindling romance. Where the problem is more serious and one or the other of the sex partners cannot function, erotic material can provide both relaxation and stimulation. Even the Meese Pornography Commission appointed by President Ronald Reagan, which was highly critical of pornography, granted in its 1986 report that it can help in "the treatment of sexual dysfunctions."[10]

It helps because it excites fantasies. This does not mean that every fantasy has to be—or indeed should be—acted out. Fantasy is fiction. Defenders of pornography remind us that while it works on our imagination, it does not cancel out the restraints on our behavior. We do not respond to sex-and-violence material by commit-ting violent sex crimes.

This is as true for children as it is for adults. They do not watch *The Wizard of Oz* and go out looking for a wicked witch to kill. They may pretend—much as adults do—by playing cops and robbers and pointing their fin-gers at each other and yelling "BANG!," but that is fantasy, game playing, not murder.

Sex Education

If we kept all knowledge of sex from children, we would be turning back the clock, say those who approve of erotica. As in the past, by keeping sex a mystery, we would make children afraid of it and increase the likelihood of their growing into adults who have problems dealing with their sexual feelings. Doctors Edward Donnerstein, Daniel Linz, and Steven Penrod offer an alternative in their book *The Question of Pornography: Research Findings and Policy Implications.* Instead of restricting children's access to sexually explicit material, they recommend "the development of educational programs that would teach viewers to become more critical consumers"[11] of it.

Of course children must be protected from real-life sex and violence say spokespeople for erotica. We have laws to do that, and people in the business of erotica are as much concerned that those laws should be enforced as Morality in Media is. Nobody in the legitimate sex industry wants to see children exploited to make kiddy porn. But they believe there is a difference between punishing someone for their sex fantasies involving children and punishing them for what they actually do. Here again, the fantasy may well be a substitute for the action, rather than a provocation leading to it. There are no crimes of thought, only crimes involving actual deeds.

It is a deed if one produces erotic material. It is a deed if one sells it. It is a deed if one buys it. But are these specific deeds—in any of these circumstances—necessarily crimes?

Child Pornography Sting Operations

The question was the central point of a 1992 case involving a Nebraska farmer named Keith Jacobson. Jacobson was convicted in federal court of "buying sexually explicit photographs of minors."[12] Before the purchase, he had been repeatedly solicited by mail to order the pictures. There was no evidence showing that Jacobson had previously had any interest in child pornography, or that he had ever attempted any sexual contact with minors.

When Jacobson's conviction was appealed, it came out that the U.S. Customs and Postal Service working with the Obscenity Unit had "entrapped"[13] Jacobson. The U.S. Supreme Court ruled that he had not been "independently predisposed to commit the crime"[14] of buying the pictures. His curiosity had been aroused and he had become the victim of a sting operation—an effort by law enforcement officers to lure him into committing a criminal act.

Nadine Strossen of the American Civil Liberties Union points out that "the kind of relentless sting operations that U.S. officials aimed at Jacobson and thousands of other individuals who had never displayed any interest in such materials made the federal government one of the major marketing forces of child porn in the U.S."[15] The U.S. Court of Appeals for the Ninth Circuit said that these sting operations sought to entrap "individuals possessing . . . a broad range of legal sexual and non-sexual interests."[16] But the fact that he had been set up did not stop Robert Brase, who was arrested for buying a kiddy-porn videotape through the mail, from committing suicide.

Both Brase and Jacobson were poor farmers. Those who believe they were unfairly entrapped believe that the crime they were accused of committing is one defined by class and status. Invariably, they point out, restrictions on pornography make class distinctions. Today, James Joyce's erotic writings and Picasso's graphically sexy sketches are available to the educated classes as literature and art. Nobody tries anymore to stop their distribution, or the distribution of woodcuts of erotic Indian temple art, or the naked *Venus de Milo*, or Voltaire's *Candide* (with its scenes of brutal disfigurement), or *Lady Chatterley's Lover*, or even such graphic accounts of sex and violence as the works of the Marquis de Sade and *The Story of O*.

A Class Distinction

But *Hustler* magazine, videocassettes featuring sex and violence, topless bars, and hard-core paperbacks, which may appeal to a rural market or blue-collar buyers with more ordinary tastes, come under constant attack from

64

those who would define the public morality. A snobbery of good taste prevails that has little to do with how erotic the content is. Opposition is based more on the quality of the work than on its pornographic content.

Their adversaries point out that this puts the leaders of the antipornography movement in the position of playing critic. They are picking and choosing and making decisions as to what is worthwhile and what is not. The problem with this is that they do not really know— nobody does—what has lasting value and what does not. Only time will determine that. Some of our most valued works of art today were considered yesterday to be not only obscene, but worthless trash. Some of the erotic works that most offend today may be classics tomorrow. Nor does such recognition have much to do with what effect such an erotic work may have on any given individual.

As Supreme Court Justice William O. Douglas pointed out in a decision involving the erotic novel *Fanny Hill*, "It would be a futile effort, even for a censor to attempt to remove all that might possibly stimulate antisocial conduct."[17] He went on to cite an example from a study on the subject in the 1964 *Wayne Law Review:*

> Heinrich Pommerenke, who was a rapist, abuser, and mass slayer of women in Germany, was prompted to his series of ghastly deeds by Cecil B. DeMille's *The Ten Commandments*. During the scene of the Jewish women dancing about the Golden Calf, all the doubts of his life came clear: Women were the source of the world's trouble and it was his mission to both punish them for this and to execute them.[18]

65

Women were his victims. But was Hollywood director Cecil B. DeMille really responsible for his terrible crimes? If not, then how responsible, really, is the seller of the most graphic sex-and-violence pornography for the crimes of the monster who may have acted on it?

That is the question dividing feminists and others concerned about pornography. And it is the question we consider next.

6

Women vs. Women: The Feminist Controversy

What should be considered pornography and what should be considered erotica is the question that lies at the heart of the feminist debate. Behind it lies a deeper question having to do with how women view men and their roles in their relationships with them. This was the question raised by Betty Friedan in her ground-breaking book *The Feminine Mystique*. The book inspired the creation in 1966 of the National Organization for Women (NOW), marking the start of the modern-day women's liberation movement in the United States.

In the 1960s, women banded together as feminists to redefine their traditional roles and to fight for equality in the workplace and the home. However, while there was some discussion of role-playing in sexual relationships, there was not much mention of pornography. That changed in the 1970s when Susan Brownmiller published *Against Our Will*, an in-depth study of rape in all its forms. It considered rape as a weapon of war, a danger in dating, a tool of courtship, a means of domination in marriage, an expression of revenge, an often tolerated and unreported crime, a matter of guilt for female victims, and a subject of humor among men. It also—and this was not its major point—discussed the role of pornography in provoking men to rape.

The book made many men defensive and furious. It bewildered many women. But quite a few heard its message in their gut and carried it to their hearts. On the whole, most of those in the women's liberation movement did not disagree with it, or at least they did not challenge it. At the time, *Against Our Will* was not recognized as the beginning of a dispute that would split feminists into two camps, but that is what it was.

It focused some feminists on the connection between pornography and sex crimes. One was a leading writer and spokesperson of the movement, Robin Morgan. "Pornography is the theory," wrote Ms. Morgan in 1977, "and rape is the practice."[1]

Women Fighting Back

It followed that if pornography was really the cause of rape, and women its most frequent victims, then something should certainly be done about pornography. This was the not unreasonable beginning of the antipornography movement among feminists. With the founding of Women Against Pornography (WAP) in New York in 1979, the movement found its most powerful voice.

68

The voice belonged to Andrea Dworkin and she quickly became a highly visible and outspoken feminist critic of pornography. She also identified who and what was responsible for it. "Pornography exists because men despise women," she told audiences, "and men despise women in part because pornography exists."[2]

If Dworkin was saying that men were the enemy, many committed feminists had difficulty accepting that. Sally O'Driscoll, writing in the *Village Voice*, called the idea "simple-minded."[3] Others were alarmed by the danger of censorship, and one critic said Dworkin possessed "an appalling historical naivete."[4]

Dworkin's zeal, though, was rooted in her personal experience. When she was eighteen years old, she had been arrested at an antiwar demonstration and subjected to a needlessly rough body-cavity search. She bled for two weeks. The incident led to calls for an investigation of the New York City Women's House of Detention.

In the late 1960s, she went to Europe. She lived in Holland for five years. There she met and married a Dutch man who physically abused her. She left him in 1971, but he followed her and continued to batter her. From such experiences came her first book, *Woman Hating*, published in 1974. One reviewer wrote that the book "awakened me to Woman as Victim in ways I never knew existed."[5]

Other feminists have said that is precisely the picture they are trying to erase. Dworkin's work, they say, keeps alive "the disempowering notion that women are essentially victims."[6] The image of women that feminism seeks to promote, they point out, is that women can be as powerful as men.

Feminists Fighting Pornography

Those who agree with Dworkin reply that power means women standing up for themselves against the pornography that not only can result in their rape, but that also demeans them as sex objects, toys for men, and exposes images of their bodies for men's pleasure. How can a young girl look at *Playboy* or *Penthouse* they ask, and regard her own body as having dignity and strength? To be exposed, to be nude, is to be made powerless. The Nazis knew that. That is one reason they stripped their victims naked before marching them to their deaths. Such images, they add, are the weapon by which men keep women in their traditionally inferior position.

One feminist antipornography group, Feminists Fighting Pornography (FFP), focused particularly on pictures in publications. Their targets were *Playboy, Penthouse*, and other more graphic skin magazines of the 1980s. Their tactic was to set up tables on busy street corners and display what they considered to be the most offensive of the magazines' photographs. People passing by were shown the erotic material and asked to sign a petition seeking laws to prohibit it.

When one of the FFP exhibitions was set up in Grand Central Station in New York City, they were ordered to remove the display because it was "disgusting"[7] to homebound commuters. FFP appealed to the New York branch of the American Civil Liberties Union (ACLU) to fight for its right to display the pornography it was trying to have banned. The ACLU, which is against restricting pornography for adults, took the case and won it.

Meanwhile, other feminists were becoming increasingly concerned. They feared the antipornography campaign was draining off energy needed to fight battles such as those for passage of the Equal Rights Amendment (ERA), for day care for the children of working mothers, against attacks on a woman's right to choose abortion, for wages equal to men's for equal work, and others. And there were also those who thought their antiporn sisters were embarking on a campaign that threatened rights of privacy, freedom of the press, and artistic expression.

Beginning of the Sex Wars

Now they too began to organize. In the beginning, WAP had claimed they were "not carving out any new exceptions to the First Amendment,"[8] meaning they were not asking for government censorship. By the early 1980s, it began to look like the antipornography feminists were after just that.

Columbia University professor Carol Vance and others founded the Feminist Anti-Censorship Taskforce (FACT). Writer Marcia Pally helped start Feminists for Free Expression (FFE) and became its president. It was the time, American Civil Liberties Union president Nadine Strossen has written, "when women who shared other feminist goals became bitterly divided over the pornography issue."[9] It was the time of the "so-called sex wars within the feminist movement."[10]

71

The sex wars exploded in 1983 when Andrea Dworkin joined forces with University of Michigan law professor Catharine MacKinnon to campaign to have laws passed to suppress pornography. Cofounder and publisher of *Ms.* magazine Gloria Steinem, a high-profile leader of the women's movement, "strongly supported these ordinances."[11] Betty Friedan and some chapters of NOW opposed them.

MacKinnon and Dworkin had both been teaching at the University of Minnesota in 1983. While there, they worked together on antipornography legislation for the Minneapolis City Council. Their work was the basis for legislation passed by the council that stated that pornography "is a practice of sex discrimination"[12] against women. It authorized lawsuits for damages against those who either sold pornography, or coerced people into posing for it or buying it. Also, it specifically authorized damages in cases of "assault or physical attack due to pornography."[13] The law defined pornography as "graphic sexually explicit subordination of women through pictures and/or words."[14]

The MacKinnon-Dworkin Act

Twice the City Council passed the MacKinnon-Dworkin Act, and twice Minneapolis Mayor Donald Fraser refused to sign it into law on the grounds that it violated the First Amendment to the Constitution. Although a new mayor replaced Fraser in 1993 and antipornography feminists have been campaigning for repassage of the law, that may not happen because of events in Indianapolis, Indiana.

In 1984, the same law was passed in Indianapolis and signed into law by Mayor William Hudnut. It was endorsed by Phyllis Schlafly, a leading antifeminist, and actively supported by Beulah Coughenour, a leader of the Indianapolis "Stop ERA" movement. This "unholy alliance with opponents of women's rights"[15] outraged many local feminists. The Indianapolis law was struck down by a federal court, and the decision was upheld by the U.S. Supreme Court. But it had seriously deepened the split over pornography in the women's movement.

Putting aside her personal feelings favoring antipornography legislation, Gloria Steinem recognized in 1985 that this was an issue with which *Ms.* had to come to grips. Mary Kay Blakely was assigned to do an article on the controversy. It was called "Is One Woman's Sexuality Another Woman's Pornography?" and it appeared in the April 1985 issue of the magazine. Blakely's account of how the article was put together illustrates just how bitter the conflict was:

> We had meetings at *Ms.* with Dworkin and MacKinnon. . . . And then we set up a similar meeting with FACT, the ACLU people, and others vs. Dworkin. The animosity between these groups became terrible. They had to meet separately because they couldn't be in the same room at the same time.[16]

One side was outraged that Dworkin and MacKinnon could ally themselves with traditional foes of the feminist movement. The other side saw their opponents as elitists out of touch with the pain pornography caused many women in America. It was not that they did not agree with traditional feminist aims centering on equality. It was that they believed the exploitation of women and the damage done to them by pornography was so much more pressing. They gained added support when Gloria Steinem wrote an article for *Ms.* about an X-rated movie performer named Linda Lovelace.

The Battering of Linda Lovelace

Lovelace was not just any porn star. She was the star of *Deep Throat*, possibly the most profitable porn film ever made. She had given many interviews telling how much she enjoyed her work as a sex star. Nora Ephron described her in an essay as "a happy and willing porn queen."[17]

But she was no such thing. As Steinem revealed in her article, Lovelace had been a virtual sex slave who was controlled and punished by her manager. "She had been beaten and raped so severely and regularly that she suffered . . . permanent injury,"[18] wrote Steinem.

The Lovelace story made it hard to defend the enjoyment of pornography by women who resented attempts to interfere with it in the name of feminism. It pulled the rug out from under those who claimed pornography was a victimless crime. Still, not all feminists were convinced that what happened to Linda Lovelace really proved anything about pornographers in general.

The ACLU's Nadine Strossen pointed out that despite the Lovelace experience there is no "reason to believe that force or violence" occurs with any greater frequency in the sex industry "than in other sectors of our society, including other workplaces and the home."[19] Candida Royalle, a top X-rated film star, told an interviewer that "I was never forced to do anything in pornography."[20] But, she added, when she had worked outside the sex industry she had on two occasions been sexually assaulted by her bosses. Another performer of sexually explicit material, Holly Hughes, believed that the laws being pushed by antipornography forces would end up being used against feminists and gay people.

The Pornography Victims' Compensation Act

Unswayed by such statements, Andrea Dworkin brought a lawsuit against *Hustler* magazine in which she asked a United States federal court to hold that pornography was not protected by the free speech provisions of the Constitution. She lost the suit, but in its wake, in 1992 in Canada, the antiporn feminists had their first major victory. The Canadian Supreme Court, influenced by a brief that Catharine MacKinnon had coauthored, decided that pornography that was "degrading," or "dehumanizing"[21] to women was against the law. Awhile later, in an unexpected turnabout, two books by Andrea Dworkin were seized at the border by Canadian authorities on the grounds that they "illegally eroticized pain and bondage."[22]

Nevertheless, versions of a MacKinnon-Dworkin-inspired bill known as the Pornography Victims' Compensation Act have been passed in Illinois and are being considered in Massachusetts, Washington, California, Wisconsin, and Suffolk County, New York. Under its provisions, any victim of a sexual assault can sue producers or distributors of pornography and collect unlimited damages if the pornography was a "substantial cause"[23] of the assault. A similar bill has been reported on favorably by the Senate Judiciary Committee, but has not yet been passed by the full Senate. Similar laws have been introduced in Germany, the Philippines, and Sweden.

Many feminists are frightened by these developments. Explaining why, Betty Friedan reminds us that *The Feminine Mystique* was once "suppressed as pornographic."[24] Author Wendy McElroy points out that "it was the state, not pornography that burned women as witches," adding that today it is still the state "that has raised barriers against women."[25]

But who else but the state, ask the antipornography feminists, will protect women from those men driven to sex crimes by pornography?

7

High Court Decisions

The average person, asking whether pornography is a crime or not, will not find consistent answers in the law. Although Supreme Court decisions are quoted by those on both sides of the debate, the law is still not clear. Indeed, it is fair to say that the Court has added to the confusion.

In 1815, when the nation's first pornography case was heard in the Pennsylvania supreme court, the strict morality of the times determined the decision. "The corruption of the public mind in general, and debauching the manners of youth in particular, by lewd and obscene pictures," it warned, would have "the most injurious consequences."[1] However, it was not this decision from a state court that set the tone for the U.S. Supreme Court in obscenity cases, but rather one from across the sea in England.

English Court's Definition of Obscenity

The case of *Regina* v. *Hicklin* (1868) was tried under the British Obscene Publications Act, which had been passed back in 1857. The act had never actually defined what obscenity was. Now the Hicklin decision established that the test of what was obscene was its tendency "to deprave and corrupt those whose minds are open to such immoral influences."[2] According to Professor Thomas I. Emerson, author of *The System of Freedom of Expression*, the Hicklin test "brought within the ban of the obscenity statutes any publication containing isolated passages that the courts felt would tend to exert an immoral influence on susceptible persons."[3]

The key phrases here are "isolated passages" and "susceptible persons." What Hicklin established was that the work as a whole did not have to be obscene to be forbidden; if one or two sentences might affect one or two people, then it could be banned. "This view," according to the *Encyclopaedia Britannica*, "was a precedent for U.S. anti-obscenity legislation, beginning with the celebrated Comstock Law of 1873."[4] It was also the guideline followed by state and federal courts at every level until the 1932 trial attempting to ban James Joyce's novel *Ulysses* from the United States on grounds of obscenity.

Judge Woolsey's decision in that trial made a distinction between what would arouse "susceptible persons" and what might excite those with "average sex instincts." It was an important distinction. Now not just anyone could determine that obscenity in a work had affected him or her. It had to have that effect on the ordinary person.

The "Dominant Effect" Standard

Two years later, a three-judge federal Appeals Court panel upheld the Woolsey decision and proposed a new standard to replace the Hicklin test. Writing for the panel, Judge Augustus Hand said that "the proper test of whether a given book is obscene is in its dominant effect."[5] He added that in order to determine that "dominant effect," the reputation of the book, how established critics rated it, and how long people had been reading it, should all be taken into consideration.

Again the ground had shifted. Again the definition of obscenity was being relaxed. Judge Hand had established "that a publication of literary merit should not be judged obscene on the basis of particular passages taken out of context."[6]

None of the cases mentioned above had involved the United States Supreme Court itself. It was not until 1957 that it became directly involved in framing standards for obscenity law. The case was *Roth* v. *United States*.

Samuel Roth had made his living publishing and distributing sexually explicit material for many years before he was indicted for using the mail system to distribute Volume 1, Number 3, of *American Aphrodite*, which contained excerpts from a much-banned work called *Venus and Tannhauser* by Aubrey Beardsley. In past years, Roth had published excerpts from *Ulysses* and *Lady Chatterley's Lover* and works by Zola and de Maupassant.

This was certainly profitable for Roth, but he also claimed to be acting on principle. He claimed that an interest in sex was healthy. Why then should people who enjoyed sexual materials not have the right to purchase them? Those who were offended, Roth pointed out, did not have to read the books he published.[7]

Roth v. *United States*: Sex vs. Obscenity

The Supreme Court did not agree that Roth had the right to publish and distribute through the mails works found to be obscene. When they handed down their decision, Justice William J. Brennan, writing for the majority, first declared that "implicit in the history of the First Amendment is the rejection of obscenity as utterly without redeeming social importance."[8] This established at the highest court level that pornography was not protected by the freedom of speech protections in the Constitution. By six to three, the high court found the Beardsley work to be obscene and upheld Roth's conviction for sending obscenity through the mails. At the age of sixty-two, Roth went to prison for five years.

The case established what came to be known as the Roth standard for obscenity. In the majority opinion, Justice Brennan pointed out that "sex and obscenity"[9] were not the same thing. He wrote that "the portrayal of sex . . . is not itself sufficient reason to deny material the constitutional protection of freedom of speech and press."[10] What was key to deciding was "whether to the average person, applying contemporary standards, the dominant theme of the material taken as a whole appeals to the prurient interest."[11] This was the Roth standard. It confused everybody, including the Supreme Court itself.

The high judges could not agree on how to apply it. Some focused on the "dominant theme," some on "contemporary standards," and some on "prurient interest."

Individual justices had trouble agreeing with each other on how one or another of these should be applied in specific cases.

As the confusion grew, there were several attempts by justices to make the guidelines clear. One of the more successful was by Justice Harlan in the 1962 case *Manual Enterprises* v. *Day*. Writing the majority opinion, he refined the "prurient interest" standard by adding that to be banned, materials must be "so offensive on their face as to affront current community standards of decency."[12]

Community and National Standards

Harlan had refined the "contemporary standards" of the Roth case to "current community standards." Since he had been dealing with a federal case, he had meant "community standards" to be national standards. However, many local and state courts hearing obscenity cases interpreted "community" to mean their own districts, or towns, and the "standards" to be local, rather than national.

There were many convictions on the grounds of "community standards." To this day the antipornography forces insist they mean local standards. The other side feels that such a view has a chilling effect on the availability of all kinds of sexual materials that may not be obscene or pornographic.

Redeeming Social Value

In 1964, *Jacobellis* v. *Ohio* added yet another requirement. Justice Brennan, in the majority opinion, wrote that in order for material to be banned, it must be

81

"utterly without redeeming social importance." This had an industry-wide effect on skin magazines like *Scamp* and *Bachelor*, which began justifying their provocative centerspreads by including serious articles on topical subjects and short stories by recognized writers like John Dos Passos and Jean Paul Sartre in order that the publication as a whole might have "social importance." According to Morality in Media, the Jacobellis decision was to a great extent responsible for the increase in pornography during the 1960s.

The confusion continued. In 1967, the U.S. Supreme Court decided three pornography cases on the same day and issued fourteen different opinions. In one of the cases, it found that the Victorian erotic novel *Fanny Hill* was not pornographic because it might have "some minimal literary value."[13] In a second case involving paperbacks mixing sex with violence, the author of one had testified that he had received "detailed instructions"[14] from publisher Edward Mishkin that "the sex had to be very strong, it had to be rough, it had to be clearly spelled out . . ."[15] None of the Court's standards excused this material and the conviction of Mishkin was upheld. But it was a third case that attracted the most attention.

The *Eros* Decision: Raunch or Race?

Ginzburg v. *United States* (1966) had been working its way through the courts since 1962 and concerned an issue of *Eros* magazine published by Ralph Ginzburg. *Eros* was a hardbound, oversized publication with glossy paper, extremely high production values, creative art direction, and quite beautiful—if often naked and explicitly sexual—photographs and illustrations. Ginzburg claimed that recent court decisions had freed publishers to be more sexually frank than ever before.

Ginzburg had tried to get mailing privileges for *Eros* from locales with names that would provide suggestive postmarks. Among the less blatant of these was Intercourse, Pennsylvania. Supreme Court Justice Brennan wrote that this showed "the leer of the sensualist." It would play a part in the Court's decision.

So would the contents of the magazine. These included a story by the French short story master Guy de Maupassant, illustrations by the renowned painter Edgar Degas, photographs of male prostitutes in Bombay, India, an article on making love with a weak heart, some seminude but otherwise rather tame French postcards, an earthy Mark Twain essay, love poetry, and "a photographic essay offering glimpses of a handsome black boy making love to a beautiful white girl."[16]

This last piece attracted the most attention. The year 1962 was the height of the civil rights struggle in the South and racially mixed couples were not a common sight in most places in America. That the white woman and the black man were nude and embracing—although not engaging in explicit lovemaking—shocked many people, black and white. Others, however, thought the photos were artistic and beautiful and said so. At Ginzburg's original trial, his attorney presented expert witnesses who testified to their artistic merit.

This evidence had been waved aside. Ginzburg was found guilty and five years later the Supreme Court upheld the verdict. They said that Ginzburg was "pandering" (a word usually applied to those who offer sex for money). This conclusion was reached in part because of his attempts to obtain suggestive postmarks. The Court explained that while the material in the magazine might not be obscene if judged on its own merits, it could be obscene "against a background of commercial exploitation of erotica solely for the sake of their prurient appeal."[17] Although Ginzburg's five-year jail sentence was upheld, he actually served only eight months.

The Supreme Court's decision caused a furor. Justice Hugo Black, disagreeing with the majority, said that Ginzburg had been punished "for distributing printed matter about sex which neither Ginzburg nor anyone else could possibly have known to be criminal."[18] Many writers, artists, lawyers, civil rights advocates, and even some antipornography crusaders protested the illogic of the Court in excusing *Fanny Hill* and convicting Ginzburg.

The Court had also done something else in the Ginzburg decision. It had said that material that was sexy but not obscene might be considered obscene if it was advertised to appeal to the buyer's interest in the obscene. This was a new standard, and it alarmed many civil libertarians. But it turned out not to be one the Court would pursue.

Actually, the Court may have reacted to all the protest over the Ginzburg case. Later in 1967, in *Redrup* v. *New York*, it said it would only uphold obscenity convictions on the basis of protecting juveniles or unwilling adults from pornography. Over the next few years, the

U.S. Supreme Court reversed a number of obscenity convictions that did not fit this definition.

The Supreme Court's Definition of Obscenity

That, of course, brought objections from those who saw it as the Court's duty to protect the public from pornography. In the landmark case *Miller* v. *California* (1973), the Court tried to spell out some standards that would strike a balance between the permissive approach of *Redrup* and the harshness of *Ginzburg*. It listed three standards by which a judge and/or a jury might determine a work or performance to be obscene and therefore not protected by the Constitution:

1. That the average person, applying contemporary community standards, would find that the work, taken as a whole, appeals to the prurient interest; and

2. That the work depicts or describes in a patently offensive way, as measured by contemporary community standards, sexual conduct specifically defined by the applicable law; and

3. That a reasonable person would find that the work, taken as a whole, lacks serious literary, artistic, political and scientific value.[19]

Chief Justice Warren Burger explained that the new standards were intended to exclude only hard-core materials from constitutional protection. However, they also did away with the "utterly without redeeming social value" definition of pornography objected to by the smut-busters. And Chief Justice Burger spelled out that a community standard did not have to be national. "It is neither realistic nor constitutionally sound to read the First Amendment as requiring that the people of Maine or Mississippi accept public depiction of conduct found tolerable in Las Vegas or New York City,"[20] wrote the Chief Justice.

That same year in *Paris Adult Theater I v. Slaton* (1973), the Court said that local government need not have conclusive scientific data that pornography was harmful in order to ban it. Nor need it have conclusive proof that there was a tie-in between porn and antisocial behavior. "The sum of experience," it said, was enough to conclude that "family life, community welfare, and the development of human personality, can be debased and distorted by crass commercial exploitation of sex."[21]

This was regarded as a victory for the antipornography forces. However, once again the Court modified its position. In 1974, it overturned a Georgia conviction that said that the film *Carnal Knowledge* was obscene. It said the film was not pornographic according to the Miller standards and added that juries did not "have unbridled discretion" to label a work pornographic.

Child Pornography Laws Upheld

By the mid-1970s, of course, the sexual revolution had profoundly changed attitudes in America. Language and acts that had once been strictly forbidden could now be seen and heard on local theater screens, and sometimes even on TV. Some things, however, were still taboo. Child pornography was one of them.

In *New York* v. *Ferber* (1982), the Supreme Court upheld a New York State law making the distribution of child pornography a crime. The particular film involved young boys committing acts of a sexual nature. The Court's decision left many questions unanswered. While it had affirmed punishment for the distributor, it had not dealt with the question of whether the film's maker, or the eventual buyer, or other adults involved with the film could be punished. It had also left vague the definition of just what constituted child pornography. It did not deal with photographs or scientific films in which children might appear naked, or photographs of children engaging in tribal rites, or the common baby-on-a-bear-rug photos taken of nude infants. There were as many loopholes as there were questions after Ferber was affirmed.

Some of them were closed in the Supreme Court's ruling in *Osborne* v. *Ohio* (1990). It established that people who possessed or viewed child pornography in their homes could be prosecuted. Justice Brennan, however, had doubts. If, he wrote, "a parent gave a family friend a picture of the parent's infant taken while the infant was unclothed, the statute would apply."[22] He also pointed out that many great painters used "models under eighteen years of age, and many acclaimed photographs and films have included nude or partially clad minors."[23] Firm definitions of kiddy porn—and any exceptions to it—have still not been established by the Supreme Court. Recently the Court's focus has switched to cases in such other areas as government funding of the arts, prime-time TV viewing by children, rap music lyrics, and regulation of sex on the Internet. These are areas that have also involved the House of Representatives and the Senate.

This is the battleground for the 1990s. On it is being determined the future status of what some call pornography and others term erotica. But if the past is any indication, it too will leave a good many questions unresolved.

8

Commissions, Regulations, Funding, and Legislation

They called it Redrupping. The term came from the Supreme Court's decision in the 1967 case *Redrup* v. *New York*, which said that only protection of minors and unwilling adults would be cause for action in pornography cases. In its wake had come reversals by the Court of many lower court obscenity convictions that did not meet the Redrup standard.

This had alarmed the antipornography forces. Organizations like Citizens for Decent Literature, religious leaders like Cardinal Francis Spellman, and United States Senators like Sam Ervin and Strom Thurmond strongly protested the permissiveness of the Court toward erotic materials and performances. Pressure was brought to bear on lawmakers to act.

The Lockhart Commission

On October 3, 1967, an act passed both houses of Congress creating a National Commission on Obscenity and Pornography "composed of eighteen members appointed by the President."[1] On January 2, 1968, President Lyndon B. Johnson named William Lockhart, dean of the law school at the University of Minnesota, to head the commission. Dean Lockhart assigned Professor Paul Bender of the University of Pennsylvania Law School to be the commission's general counsel. Professor Bender had been the lawyer who argued the government's case against Ralph Ginzburg before the Supreme Court.

For two years the commission, which had only two female members, gathered evidence, conducted investigations, and met for discussions. On September 30, 1970, it submitted its report to Congress and to President Richard Nixon. The commission found no link between pornography and sex crime. It recommended scrapping laws against the distribution of obscene materials,[2] but said there might be narrowly focused laws regulating specific materials and circumstances, particularly where children were involved. It also urged "that the country get serious about sex education."[3]

Negative reaction to the report was immediate. President Nixon denounced the commission as "morally bankrupt."[4] West Virginia Senator Robert Byrd said the report indicated that the nation was immoral.[5] Vice President Spiro Agnew assured the public that "Main Street is not going to become Smut Alley."[6]

Three members of the commission dissented from the report. One was Charles H. Keating, Jr., who had been a founding member of Citizens for Decent Literature. The two others—Catholic clergyman Father Morton A. Hill and Dr. Winfrey C. Link—issued a minority report. It contained some two dozen recommendations for regulating pornography "by constitutional means."[7] Among them were suggestions for standards to license and enforce the licensing of motion pictures, definitions of subject matter to be classified as "obscene for minors,"[8] and guidelines for prosecution of "every person who sings or speaks any obscene song . . . in any play, night club act . . . or in any public place."[9]

Neither the Hill-Link minority report nor the Lockhart committee majority report resulted in legislation by Congress. Over the following years, the manufacture and distribution of sexually explicit materials and the staging of erotic performances continued to increase. So too did the opposition to it.

The Meese Commission

Finally, in February 1985, President Ronald Reagan took action. "We had identified the worst hazardous waste sites in America," he said. "It was about time we did the same with the worst sources of pornography."[10] He established the Attorney General's Commission on Pornography, headed by Attorney General Edwin Meese. Its purpose was to measure the effects of pornography on the people of the United States, and to figure out ways to stop it from spreading without stepping on rights guaranteed by the Constitution.

The eleven-member committee was immediately attacked by anticensorship forces. Just as the members of the Lockhart Commission had been accused of tuning out any evidence that would have led to the limiting of pornography, now members of the Meese Commission were accused of having been picked because of their antipornography opinions. Barry Lynn of the ACLU complained that not one Meese Commission member questioned the link between pornography and violence, or wondered how laws banning pornography might violate the First Amendment.

Nevertheless, the Meese Commission held hearings in cities around the country. It took testimony from 208 witnesses. It collected letters and written statements regarding "pornography-related victimization."[11] A little more than a year after it had been formed, the commission issued its report.

They were unanimous in their conclusions. "Substantial exposure to sexually violent materials," they found, "bears a causal relationship to antisocial acts of sexual violence . . . and [causes] an increase in aggressive behavior directed toward women."[12] They also noted that "substantial exposure to materials of this type" contributed to "non-violent forms of discrimination against . . . women."[13] They said it was "important to examine the developmental patterns of offenders"[14] and pornography's effects on them. And they called for "more strict legal measures"[15] to punish those involved with pornography.

The commission defined pornography as "material that is predominantly sexually explicit and intended

primarily for the purpose of sexual arousal."[16] The Meese
Report itself fell short of that, but it was quite graphic. It
included an explicit eleven-page abridgment of the script
of the X-rated film *Deep Throat*. Professor Walter
Kendrick of Fordham University, author of *The Secret
Museum*, a study of pornography, called the report "bla-
tantly pornographic."[17] *Newsweek* magazine said it was
"the Attorney General's Dirty Book."[18]

The Child Protection and Obscenity Enforcement Act

To others, however, the Meese Report was a shocking
exposé of the depths to which pornography was dragging
down the country. Religious organizations of evangelical
Christians, conservative Catholics, and Orthodox Jews
called for government action. The Justice Department
responded by drafting the Child Protection and
Obscenity Enforcement Act, which was unveiled by
President Ronald Reagan on November 10, 1987.

President Reagan pointed out that pornography had
"expanded into new areas employing new technologies
and reaching new audiences." He said that "respect for
common decency and human suffering" demanded
action. And he praised "the creation of the National
Obscenity Enforcement Unit" as the "centerpiece"[19] of a
seven-point plan by the attorney general to fight
pornography.

The Child Protection and Obscenity Enforcement
Act was passed by the Senate on October 21, 1988, and
signed into law by President Reagan on November 18,
1988. In March 1989, a coalition made up of the

American Library Association, the Freedom to Read Foundation, the Council for Periodical Distributors, and the American Booksellers Association brought an action against Attorney General Dick Thornburgh to stop him from enforcing the act. On May 23, 1987, the Washington, D.C., Federal District Court ruled that the act was unconstitutional. In 1990, Congress amended the law to deal with its constitutional shortcomings. Nevertheless, a Washington, D.C., district court again found the amended act unconstitutional in 1992. The government appealed and in 1994, the Washington, D.C., Court of Appeals overturned the decision of the lower court and said the revised act was constitutional. The other side appealed that decision to the Supreme Court. In June 1995, the Supreme Court refused to hear that appeal, and so the decision of the Court of Appeals stands and the amended Child Protection and Obscenity Enforcement Act is now the law of the land.

The Pornography Victims' Compensation Act

Hearings were held on another bill, the Pornography Victims' Compensation Act mentioned in Chapter 6, by the Senate Committee on the Judiciary in July 1991. One of the first people the Committee took testimony from was Robert H. Macy, district attorney of Oklahoma City and then president-elect of the National DA's Association. "In Oklahoma County, in 1984," he told the committee, "we started a five year crackdown on pornography and sex oriented businesses. Five years later,

94

we had experienced a 24.4 percent reduction in reported rapes. The evidence speaks for itself."[20]

The bill made it possible for victims to collect damages from producers or distributors of pornography that had provoked a sexual assault against them. This, testified president of the American Booksellers Association Joyce Meskis, would "produce the most pervasive censorship the U.S. has ever experienced."[21] Anne Rice, author of *Interview with the Vampire*, called the proposed legislation "evil" and pointed out that if a victim can sue a magazine for provoking her rape, then the rapist can claim, "'It was the magazine that made me do it, and it was also the way she was dressed.' Why can't he sue her?"[22]

The National Endowment for the Arts Controversy

Although the committee recommended passage by the full Senate, the Pornography Victims' Compensation Act fell between the cracks when the antiporn spotlight turned to focus on the National Endowment for the Arts (NEA). The NEA awards grants of federal money to promote the arts in the United States. In 1989, the NEA came under attack because of a grant to a Washington, D.C., gallery to exhibit the works of photographer-artist Robert Mapplethorpe.

Mapplethorpe was a gay man who had died of AIDS, and much of his work was erotic. Both his lifestyle and his pictures offended Senator Jesse Helms of North Carolina. Helms said that Mapplethorpe had used "his talent to promote homosexuality," adding that "this nation is on the slippery slope in terms of morals and decency."[23]

The time had come, Senator Helms said, for Congress to supervise NEA funding of the arts. He was supported by Senator Alphonse D'Amato of New York, who said the question was "whether American taxpayers should be forced to support such trash."[24] TV talk show host and writer William F. Buckley, Jr., agreed. "If a democratic society cannot find a way to protect a taxpaying Christian heterosexual from . . . subsidizing blasphemous acts," he observed, "then democracy isn't working."[25]

Robert Mapplethorpe had grown up about twenty miles from Manhattan, where he attended art school. There he began making collages using photos and drawings from pornographic magazines. Mapplethorpe once told an interviewer that pornography was acceptable if it was good.

Just how good was Mapplethorpe? Very good indeed, according to many art critics. His pictures are in the permanent collections of the National Gallery of Art, the National Museum of American Art, and the Chicago Art Institute. New York's Whitney Museum of American Art has devoted two major shows to his work.

This did not stop Senator Jesse Helms from introducing a Senate bill in July 1989 to set up supervision over the awarding of NEA money. The bill drew immediate support from the American Family Association. Its 380,000 members and 178,000 affiliated churches were furious about an NEA-sponsored exhibit featuring a photograph by Andres Serrano of a small plastic crucifix. The crucifix had been immersed in urine.

People of every denomination were outraged. Serrano tried to explain, saying it represented his ambivalent feelings about religion. He spoke of a minister's wife telling him how moved she and her husband had been by the work.

Art or Smut? Deciding Who Pays

The issue in Congress was whether taxpayers should have to support art like Mapplethorpe's and Serrano's. There was a suggestion that the NEA be put out of business. But there were cries of censorship from the other side. The human body and its functions had always been subjects for art, they claimed. If the NEA could be made to withhold money because of breaches of good taste, it would stifle creativity.

Nevertheless, on October 7, 1989, a Senate-House bill requiring the NEA's chairperson to not fund any art project he or she judged obscene was unanimously enacted into law. The standards spelled out by the Supreme Court in the 1973 Miller case were to be the guidelines. As a result, in 1990 four grants to sexually controversial performance artists that had received unanimous approval from the NEA judges were canceled.

The ACLU, the Center for Constitutional Rights, and the National Campaign for Freedom of Expression sued on behalf of the artists. In 1992, federal court Judge A. Wallace Tashima ruled that "the fact that the exercise of professional judgment is inescapable in arts funding does not mean that the government has free rein to impose whatever content restrictions it chooses." In June 1993, the grants to the four performance artists were restored. Just prior to that, the Justice Department had asked a federal Court of Appeals to overturn Judge Tashima's ruling, but the appeal was never pursued.

During the 1990s, Congress repeatedly slashed the NEA budget. This influenced many museums, galleries, theater groups, writers, artists, and others who are dependent on NEA funding to censor themselves. Others also imposed self-censorship in the climate of disapproval of sexually explicit works created by the NEA battles.

The 2 Live Crew Case

One group that had never censored itself was the rap group 2 Live Crew. Their album *As Nasty As They Wanna Be* had already sold nearly 2 million copies by the summer of 1989 when a Fort Lauderdale, Florida, record shop owner was arrested, tried, and convicted for selling it. A week later, when 2 Live Crew appeared in Fort Lauderdale, three of its four members were arrested on obscenity charges.

The lyrics they sang were sexually explicit. The lyrics also urged male dominance over women. In *U.S. News & World Report*, columnist John Leo wrote that because of their influence "10- and 12-year-old boys now walk down the street chanting about the joys of"[26] sexually brutalizing little girls.

At the 2 Live Crew trial, defense witnesses testified that the group's songs had artistic and political value. One critic traced the history of hip-hop music. Another explained it in terms of an African-American tradition of humor not meant to be taken literally. The three accused rap musicians were found not guilty. Since that time, objections to rap music lyrics—and specifically to gangsta rap (rap that uses frank language meant as an assault)—have increased. Both ordinary crimes and sex crimes have been blamed on it. On May 31, 1995, Republican presidential candidate Senator Bob Dole attacked "music extolling the pleasures of raping, torturing and mutilating women."[27] He blasted the entertainment industry, saying that "our popular culture threatens to undermine our character as a nation."[28] He accused such films as *Natural Born Killers* and *True Romance*, and rap groups like Cannibal Corpose, Geto Boys, and 2 Live Crew of glorifying "mindless violence and loveless sex."[29]

Oliver Stone, who directed *Natural Born Killers*, said it was "the height of hypocrisy for Senator Dole, who wants to repeal the assault weapons ban, to blame Hollywood for the violence in our society."[30] Mark Canton, chairman of Columbia-TriStar, said that the issue was one of "creative rights."[31] And Lara Bergthold, executive director of the Hollywood Women's Political Committee, called Dole's speech "unbelievable hypocrisy."[32]

But Dole's attack also had many supporters. One was columnist Jonathan Yardley, writing in the Raleigh, North Carolina, *News & Observer* the following week. Yardley framed the question for people who were offended as Dole was, but who also were concerned with the "creative rights" question. "As consumers of mass entertainment, all of us are part of the problem," wrote Yardley. "What can we do to clean up our popular culture without violating rights that all of us treasure?"[33]

Regulating the Tube

One area in which the question is being addressed is television. Back in the 1992 presidential campaign, Vice President Dan Quayle had raised it in regard to "family values"[34] being undermined by the permissiveness of sitcoms like *Murphy Brown*. He had been offended by the show's approving attitude toward unmarried Murphy's becoming a single mother.

At that time the Federal Communications Commission (FCC) had been trying to expand enforcement against indecency on TV, but the courts had rejected their approach. They had also said a law passed by Congress that imposed a round-the-clock ban on indecent programming was not legal. Congress passed a second law dealing with the problem in 1992. This one allowed broadcasters to carry such programming between midnight and 6:00 A.M., but not between 6:00 A.M. and 10:00 P.M. The FCC introduced new regulations in 1993.

Both the law and the regulations were challenged. On June 30, 1995, the federal Court of Appeals for the District of Columbia rejected the challenge and said the government had a "compelling interest"[35] in protecting children. On January 9, 1996, the Supreme Court let the decision of the Court of Appeals stand.

Among those who disagreed was Chief Judge Harry T. Edwards, one of the four dissenters from the Court of Appeals decision. He thought the ruling "conflicts with the rights of parents to rear their children in the way they see fit."[36] But Congress once again thought otherwise—and this time overwhelmingly.

100

One of the provisions of a major telecommunications bill passed by both houses of Congress on February 1, 1996, is that television set manufacturers "must include in sets a *V chip* that can be used to filter out violent or sexually oriented programs if broadcasters code them as such."[37] The V chip would be controlled by parents who would program it. Television programmers were to "devise a rating system"[38] to go with the V chip. The bill passed the Senate by a vote of 91 to 5 and the House approved it by 414 to 16. President Clinton immediately announced that he would sign it. However, free speech advocates led by the ACLU were just as quick to announce that they would challenge the legality of the V chip.

The International Cyberporn Battle

The part of the telecommunications bill having to do with the Internet is even more controversial. The reason is a new worldwide phenomenon known as cyberporn. In July 1995, a study released by "a research team at Carnegie Mellon University in Pittsburgh" had surveyed 917,410 "sexually explicit pictures, descriptions, short stories and film clips." It concluded that 83.5 percent "were pornographic"[39] and hard-core. The Carnegie study was later challenged by Professor Donna Hoffman of Vanderbilt University, who said it "contains serious conceptual, logical and methodological flaws and errors."[40]

Nevertheless, the study had aroused concerns over cyberporn. This led Senator Jim Exon of Nebraska to introduce the Communications Decency Act to be included in the telecommunications bill when it was first being considered. At that time Speaker of the House Newt Gingrich had voiced doubts about it. His concern was protecting free speech for adults and at the same time protecting children when both have access to the Internet. However, the Senate approved including the Communications Decency Act in the telecommunications bill by a vote of eighty-four to sixteen. Senator Patrick Leahy of Vermont was one of the sixteen in opposition.

Leahy had favored an approach that would allow parents themselves to protect their children. This was practical thanks to software similar to the television V chip being developed by three manufacturers. The software could be keyed into a rating system similar to movie ratings. Parents would be able to screen out objectionable materials based on the ratings. But the Senate had voted not to hold hearings on the new technology.

During the first week of January 1996, the controversy over sex on the Internet shifted to Germany. The German courts asked CompuServe, which is an on-line provider for the Internet, to block the availability in Germany of some two hundred on-line discussion groups and picture databases that violated that country's pornography laws. According to *Time* magazine, among the two hundred are "sexuality support groups for the handicapped and a bulletin board for homosexuals that has served as a lifeline for thousands of gay youth."[41]

CompuServe responded that it could not satisfy the German demand without pulling the plug on the objectionable programs throughout its worldwide system. The passage on February 2, 1996, of the United States telecommunications bill makes that outcome much more likely. The "bill prohibits transmission of material deemed indecent over computer networks, imposing serious penalties on those who knowingly send such materials to minors."[42]

The word "indecent" was like a red flag to a bull where civil liberties groups were concerned. In the past, courts had judged material *indecent* if it had redeeming social value and allowed it, while *obscene* material had been banned. "The standard is unconstitutional,"[43] protested Washington, D.C., communications lawyer Robert Butler. "The Internet has been given second-class speech rights,"[44] said Jerry Berman, director of the Center for Democracy and Technology, which challenged the provision in the courts.

Although the Communications Decency Act, as the bill is now known, was signed into law by President Clinton, a federal district court did indeed recently find it unconstitutional. As of this writing, the Justice Department plans to appeal that ruling to the Supreme Court.

The Internet battle centers on just how dangerous the objectionable material may be to children. Should all Internet users be deprived of programming in order to protect some Internet users—children specifically—from it? Is it worth the price?

9

Afterword

Children are a major focus of all the controversies surrounding what some call pornography and others regard as erotica. To what extent should these young people be protected? At what age? Who should decide what they should be shielded from and what they should be allowed to see? The lawmakers? The courts? The police? Religious leaders? Teachers? Parents?

From just how much should young people be protected? Should books that offend be taken out of school libraries? Should outlets for X-rated videocassettes and obscene picture magazines be prevented from operating near neighborhood schools? Should museums and art galleries restrict what they exhibit because children may see it? Should purchasers of kiddy porn be jailed because minors have been exploited in producing it? Should young people be prevented from buying rap recordings with lyrics that provoke sex and violence? Should objectionable material on TV be limited during certain hours so that minors cannot see it? Should Dial-A-Porn be made illegal to guard the young against exposure to it? Should erotic chat groups on the Internet be forbidden to safeguard children from sexual predators who make contact through them?

What about sex education? Is it pornography in disguise? If not, should it be taught in the schools? If it is taught, at what point do the illustrations used in teaching it become so sexually explicit as to be considered pornographic? Who decides? The teacher? The parents? The young people themselves?

How and Why Young People React

Many considerations affect how young people react to erotic materials. How stable is their family situation? How have they been raised to regard women? What is the attitude in the family toward discipline and punishment and violence? How do their role models—fathers or some other male for boys; mothers or some other woman for girls—behave toward the opposite sex? Are erotic materials allowed in the home? What is the attitude toward them?

Nor is the home situation the only consideration. What about friends? Is pornography shared among them? Does peer pressure among young men glorify violence and negative attitudes toward women? Does it encourage premarital sex with all the dangers that may involve? Are young people of both sexes being affected by the sheer volume of sexually explicit material in movie theaters, on television screens, in magazines, and in the music to which they listen?

It cannot be denied that there is more erotica out in the open today than ever before. Some view that as destroying youth. They point to a rising number of unmarried teenage mothers and a rising teenage sex-crime rate as evidence of the harm being done. Young people lead their list of the victims of pornography.

Others view the increase in erotica as a reflection of the society—an effect, not a cause—and not necessarily harmful. They see the modern openness toward sex where young people are concerned as both honest and healthy. Yesterday, they say, when all sex was in the closet, guilt and unhappiness among young people was widespread. Exposure to sexually explicit materials helps do away with such feelings among the young.

Being Part of the Solution

The truth may be that some young people are more ready than others to deal with sexually explicit materials. But the same is true of adults. Not everybody who is disgusted by pornography is repressed. Not everybody who is attracted to it is sick. Among the young, as among their elders, there is a wide range of reactions and attitudes to pornography.

Like their elders, some young people think all pornography should be banned. Others believe there should be no restrictions on erotic materials. Many favor a middle course that would be sensitive to that which offends without trespassing on the rights of others.

Probably many young people are as confused about just what that course should be as adults are.

Nevertheless, the day will come when young people will have to deal with the problem themselves rather than have their elders deal with it for them. They will have to decide whether to call it pornography, or erotica, and what to do about it. They will have to decide what is best for *their* children.

Hopefully, when that day comes, this book will have been of some help.

Chronology

1455—Gutenberg invents the printing press. Books— including pornography—can be mass produced.

1802—In England, the Society for the Suppression of Vice bans works that might arouse the passions of the poor.

1815—First United States pornography case is heard in the Pennsylvania Supreme Court.

1818—Dr. Thomas Bowdler censors the works of Shakespeare.

1833—The American wordsmith Noah Webster bowdlerizes the Bible.

1857—Obscene Publications Bill is passed in England.

1868—British case, *Regina* v. *Hicklin*, sets the precedent for United States pornography law.

1873—New York Society for the Suppression of Vice is formed; Comstock Act is passed.

1888—Henry Vizetelly is tried and convicted for publishing Emile Zola's novel *La Terre.*

1913—Anthony Comstock prosecutes *September Morn.*

1921—Movie companies set up the Hays Office to oversee Hollywood morality.

1925—Theodore Dreiser's *An American Tragedy* is banned in Massachusetts.

1932—Judge John M. Woolsey rules that James Joyce's *Ulysses* is not obscene.

1934—The Hays Office institutes the Production Code with strict antisex standards.

1953—*The Moon is Blue* is released without a Production Code Seal of Approval and Hollywood censorship is over.

1953—The first issue of *Playboy* is published.

1957—In *Roth* v. *United States*, the Supreme Court says the First Amendment does not cover obscenity.

1961—Lenny Bruce is arrested for the first time for using obscene language.

1962—The Supreme Court says "community standards" determine what is obscene.

1967—*Fanny Hill* is deemed not pornographic because it has "minimal literary value."

1967—Supreme Court rules that *Eros* magazine with pictures of interracial nudity is obscene and that the publisher is guilty of pandering.

1970—The Lockhart Commission finds no connection between pornography and sex crime; President Nixon rejects their findings.

1973—The Supreme Court defines obscenity standards in *Miller* v. *California*.

1982—The Court upholds the constitutionality of an antichild pornography law.

1983—Antipornography law drafted by Andrea Dworkin and Catharine MacKinnon is passed in Minneapolis.

1987—The Child Protection and Obscenity Enforcement Act, inspired by the findings of the Meese Commission, is signed into law by President Reagan.

1989—The National Endowment for the Arts comes under attack for financing an exhibition of the works of photographer Robert Mapplethorpe.

1989—Popular rap group 2 Live Crew is acquitted of singing obscene lyrics.

1990—Antichild pornography laws are strengthened by Supreme Court's ruling in *Osborne* v. *Ohio*.

1994—Revised version of the Child Protection and Obscenity Enforcement Act is upheld when the Supreme Court refuses to consider an appeal.

1995—Presidential candidate Senator Robert Dole blasts the entertainment industry for glorifying sex and violence.

1996—Landmark communications bill passed by both houses of Congress says TV set manufacturers must provide a V chip to shield children from sex and violence. The bill also bars indecency from the Internet.

Chapter Notes

Chapter 1

1. *Webster's New Universal Unabridged Dictionary* (New York: Dorset & Baber, 1983), p. 1402.
2. Ibid.
3. Ibid., p. 1234.
4. Ibid.
5. Nadine Strossen, *Defending Pornography: Free Speech, Sex, and the Fight for Women's Rights* (New York: Scribner, 1995), p. 53.

Chapter 2

1. G.L. Simons, *Simons' Book of World Sexual Records* (New York: Amjon Publishers Inc., 1976), p. 345.
2. Ibid.
3. Ova Brusendorff and Poul Henningsen, *Love's Picture Book: Vol. IV, The History of Pleasure and Moral Indignation*, trans. Elsa Gress (New York: Lyle Stuart, 1969), p. 31.
4. *Encyclopaedia Britannica*, Book III (Chicago: Encyclopaedia Britannica Inc., 1984), p. 1084.
5. *Encyclopaedia Britannica*, Book II, p. 204.
6. Simons, p. 400.
7. Ibid.
8. Edward De Grazia, *Girls Lean Back Everywhere: The Law of Obscenity and the Assault on Genius* (New York: Random House, 1992), p. 40.
9. Ibid., p. 43.
10. Carl Sifakis, *The Encyclopedia of American Crime* (New York: Facts on File, 1982), p. 650.
11. Simons, p. 180.
12. Ibid.
13. Ibid.
14. De Grazia, p. 5.
15. Ibid.

16. Sifakis, p. 165.
17. Ibid., p. 164.
18. Ibid.
19. Ibid., p. 165.
20. Ibid., p. 650.
21. Ibid., p. 165.
22. De Grazia, p. 6.
23. *Encyclopaedia Britannica*, Book V, p. 618.
24. De Grazia, p. 11.
25. Ibid., p. 133.
26. Ibid., p. 31.
27. Ibid.
28. Nat Hentoff, *Free Speech for Me—But Not for Thee* (New York: HarperCollins, 1992), p. 325.

Chapter 3

1. Carlos Fuentes, *The Buried Mirror: Reflections on Spain and the New World* (Boston: Houghton Mifflin Company, 1992), p. 225.
2. Nadine Strossen, *Defending Pornography: Free Speech, Sex, and the Fight for Women's Rights* (New York: Scribner, 1995), p. 22, picture inset following p. 160.
3. G.L. Simons, *Simons' Book of World Sexual Records* (New York: Amjon Publishers Inc., 1976), p. 348.
4. Ibid.
5. Kenneth Anger, *Hollywood Babylon* (New York: Dell Paperbacks, 1981), p. 24.
6. Ibid.
7. Ibid., p. 26.
8. Ibid., p. 56.
9. Simons, p. 380.
10. Scott Siegel and Barbara Siegel, *The Encyclopedia of Hollywood* (New York: Facts on File, 1990), p. 189.
11. Ibid., p. 189.
12. Leta W. Clark, *Women, Women, Women: Quips, Quotes and Commentary* (New York: Drake Publishers Inc., 1977), p. 100.
13. Simons, p. 381.
14. Siegel and Siegel, p. 189.
15. Simons, p. 360.

16. Ibid., p. 361.

17. Ibid.

18. Ibid.

19. Ibid.

20. Russell Shaw, "Washington: Step Right Up to the Peep Show," *Columbia: Knights of Columbus Magazine*, June 1995, p. 5.

21. Ibid.

22. Associated Press, "Unfit for Prime Time," *Newsday*, January 9, 1996, p. A16.

23. Ibid.

24. Edmund Andrews, "Court Upholds a Ban on 'Indecent' Broadcast Programming," *The New York Times*, July 1, 1995, p. 7.

Chapter 4

1. Walter Kendrick, *The Secret Museum: Pornography in Modern Culture* (New York: Viking, 1987), pp. 144–145.

2. Archbishop John P. Foley, "Critic & Teacher," *Columbia: Knights of Columbus Magazine*, June 1995, pp. 6–7.

3. *Pornography and Violence in the Communications Media: A Pastoral Response* (Philadelphia: Report of the Pontifical Council for Social Communications, 1989).

4. Harold Schelhter, "A Movie Made Me Do It," *The New York Times*, December 3, 1995, p. E15.

5. Richard McMunn, "Silence Isn't Golden," *Columbia: Knights of Columbus Magazine,* June 1995, p. 18.

6. William Bole, "The Damage is Done," *Columbia: Knights of Columbus Magazine*, June 1995, p. 9.

7. Ibid.

8. Ibid.

9. McMunn, p. 17.

10. Edward De Grazia, *Girls Lean Back Everywhere: The Law of Obscenity and the Assault on Genius* (New York: Random House, 1992), p. 555.

11. Russell Shaw, "Step Right Up to the Peep Show," *Columbia: Knights of Columbus Magazine*, June 1995, p. 5.

12. Dr. Victor B. Cline, *Pornography's Effects on Adults & Children* (New York: Morality in Media, 1995), p. 8.

13. Kenneth S. Kantzer, "Pornography Affects Teen Sexuality," in *Teenage Sexuality: Opposing Viewpoints* (San Diego: Greenhaven Press, Inc., 1994), p. 48.

14. Bernard Casserly, "The Time of Our Lives," *Columbia: Knights of Columbus Magazine*, June 1995, p. 14.

15. Ibid.

16. Kantzer, p. 47.

17. Ibid.

18. Cline, p. 10.

19. Patricia Chargot, "Don't Touch! Children and Sex," *The New York Daily News*, July 9, 1989, p. 4.

20. Ibid.

21. Daryl F. Gates and Ralph W. Bennett, "The Relationship Between Pornography and Extrafamilial Child Sexual Abuse," *The Police Chief Magazine*, February 1991, p. 15.

22. "Censorship," a Morality in Media flyer.

23. Ibid.

Chapter 5

1. Bishop Donald Wuerl, "The Fall from Grace," *Columbia: Knights of Columbus Magazine*, June 1995, p. 12.

2. *The Report of the Commission on Obscenity and Pornography* (1970), p. 31.

3. Edward De Grazia, *Girls Lean Back Everywhere: The Law of Obscenity and the Assault on Genius* (New York: Random House, 1992), p. 554.

4. Ibid.

5. Author's interview, December 19, 1995.

6. Benjamin Kyle, *Qaddafi* (New York: Chelsea House, 1987), p. 36.

7. Pete Hamill, "Women on the Verge of a Legal Breakdown," *Playboy*, January 1993, p. 189.

8. Nadine Strossen, *Defending Pornography: Free Speech, Sex, and the Fight for Women's Rights* (New York: Scribner, 1995), p. 163.

9. Susan Sontag, "The Pornographic Imagination," in *Styles of Radical Will* (New York: Anchor Books, 1969), p. 36.

10. Strossen, p. 163.

11. Nat Hentoff, *Free Speech for Me—But Not for Thee* (New York: HarperCollins, 1992), p. 346.

12. Strossen, p. 95.

13. United States Supreme Court: *Jacobson* v. *United States* (1992), p. 112.

14. Ibid.

15. Strossen, p. 95.

16. United States Court of Appeals, Fifth Circuit: *United States* v. *Mitchell* (1990), p. 915.

17. Hentoff, p. 348.

18. Ibid.

Chapter 6

1. Robin Morgan, *Going Too Far: The Personal Chronicle of a Feminist* (New York: Random House, 1977), p. 169.

2. *Current Biography*, October 1994, p. 149.

3. Ibid.

4. Ibid.

5. Jeanne Kinney, review in *Best Sellers*, July 1, 1974.

6. Nadine Strossen, *Defending Pornography: Free Speech, Sex, and the Fight for Women's Rights* (New York: Scribner, 1995), p. 245.

7. Ibid., p. 72.

8. Ibid., p. 73.

9. Ibid.

10. Ibid.

11. Carolyn G. Heilbrun, *The Education of a Woman: The Life of Gloria Steinem* (New York: The Dial Press, 1995), p. 259.

12. Andrea Dworkin and Catharine MacKinnon, *Pornography and Civil Rights: A New Day for Women's Equality* (Minneapolis: Organizing Against Pornography, 1988), p. 138.

13. Ibid.

14. Ibid.

15. Strossen, p. 78.

16. Heilbrun, pp. 261–262.

17. Ibid., p. 345.

18. Ibid.

19. Strossen, p. 190.

20. Ibid.

21. Ibid., p. 19.

22. Ibid., p. 237.

23. Ibid., p. 64.

24. Ibid., p. 199.

25. Wendy McElroy, "The Unholy Alliance," *Liberty*, February 1993, p. 53.

Chapter 7

1. Author unknown, *Summary of Laws Against Obscenity and Pornography* (New York: Morality in Media, 1995), p. 5. Quoting *Commonwealth* v. *Sharpless* (Pennsylvania Supreme Court, 1815).

2. *Encyclopaedia Britannica,* Book VII (Chicago: Encyclopaedia Britannica Inc., 1984), p. 466.

3. Thomas I. Emerson, *The System of Freedom of Expression* (New York: Random House, Vintage Books, 1970), p. 469.

4. *Encyclopaedia Britannica,* Book VII, p. 466.

5. Elder Witt, ed., *The Supreme Court and Individual Rights* (Washington, D.C.: Congressional Quarterly Inc., 1980), p. 56.

6. Ibid.

7. Edward De Grazia, *Girls Lean Back Everywhere: The Law of Obscenity and the Assault on Genius* (New York: Random House, 1992), p. 280.

8. Witt, p. 56.

9. Ibid.

10. Ibid.

11. Ibid.

12. United States Supreme Court: *Manual Enterprises* v. *Day* (1962), p. 370.

13. United States Supreme Court: *A Book Named "John Cleland's Memoirs of a Woman of Pleasure"* v. *Attorney General of Massachusetts* (1966), p. 383.

14. United States Supreme Court: *Mishkin* v. *New York* (1966), pp. 560–561.

15. Ibid.

16. Merle Miller, "Ralph Ginzburg, Middlesex, N.J. and the First Amendment," *The New York Times Magazine*, April 30, 1972, p. 67.

17. Witt, p. 57.
18. De Grazia, p. 511.
19. *Summary of Laws Against Obscenity and Pornography*, p. 2.
20. Witt, p. 57.
21. *Summary of Laws Against Obscenity and Pornography*, p. 3.
22. De Grazia, p. 582.
23. Ibid.

Chapter 8

1. Fr. Morton A. Hill and Dr. Winfrey C. Link, *The Hill Link Minority Report of the Presidential Commission on Obscenity and Pornography* (New York: Morality in Media, Undated), unnumbered p. 5 (Reprint of *Public Law 90-100*).

2. Edward De Grazia, *Girls Lean Back Everywhere: The Law of Obscenity and the Assault on Genius* (New York: Random House, 1992), p. 552.

3. Ibid.
4. Ibid.
5. Ibid.
6. Ibid.
7. Hill and Link.
8. Ibid., p. 507.
9. Ibid., p. 465.
10. De Grazia, p. 584.
11. Ibid.

12. Dr. Victor B. Cline, *Pornography's Effects on Adults & Children* (New York: Morality in Media, 1995), p. 8.

13. Ibid.

14. M.K. Condron and J.E. Nutter, Study in *Journal of Sex & Marital Therapy*, vol. 14, 1988, p. 285.

15. D. Linz, "The Findings and Recommendations of the Attorney General's Commission on Pornography: Do the Psychological 'Facts' Fit the Political Fury?" *American Psychology*, vol. 42, 1987, p. 946.

16. Author unknown, *Summary of Laws Against Obscenity and Pornography* (New York: Morality in Media, 1995), p. 2.

17. Walter Kendrick, *The Secret Museum: Pornography in Modern Culture* (New York: Viking, 1987), p. 234.

18. Nadine Strossen, *Defending Pornography: Free Speech, Sex, and the Fight for Women's Rights* (New York: Scribner, 1995), p. 157.

19. De Grazia, p. 763.

20. Hearing Before the Committee on the Judiciary, United States Senate, on *The Pornography Victims' Compensation Act of 1991,* July 23, 1991 (Washington, D.C.: U.S. Government Printing Office, 1992), p. 220.

21. Strossen, p. 68.

22. Digby Diehl, "Anne Rice," *Playboy,* March 1993, p. 56.

23. *The New York Times,* July 28, 1989, p. A11.

24. Carol S. Vance, "The War on Culture," *Art in America,* September 1989, p. 41.

25. *ARTnews,* October 1989, p. 139.

26. De Grazia, p. 657.

27. Bernard Weinraub, "Films & Records Threaten Social Fabric, Dole Asserts," *The New York Times,* June 1, 1995, p. B10.

28. Ibid., p. A1.

29. Ibid., p. B10.

30. Bernard Weinraub, "Filmmakers Discount Criticism by Dole," *The New York Times,* June 2, 1995, p. A24.

31. Ibid.

32. Weinraub, "Films & Records Threaten Social Fabric, Dole Asserts," p. B10.

33. Jonathan Yardley, "Bob Dole Gives Hollywood a Negative Review," *Raleigh News & Observer,* June 7, 1995, p. 11A.

34. Weinraub, "Films & Records Threaten Social Fabric, Dole Asserts," p. B10.

35. Edmund L. Andrews, "Court Upholds a Ban on 'Indecent' Broadcast Programming," *The New York Times,* July 1, 1995, p. 7.

36. Ibid.

37. Jeanne Dugan Cooper and Susan Benkelman, "It's Revolutionary," *Newsday,* February 2, 1996, p. A7.

38. Bill Carter, "The Network Sees Potential for Growth," *The New York Times,* February 2, 1996, p. D6.

39. Author unknown, "Not So Naughty," *New Republic,* July 31, 1995, p. 11.

40. Ibid.

41. "Pulling the Plug on Porn," *Time*, January 8, 1996, p. 62.

42. Cooper and Benkelman, p. A7.

43. Ibid.

44. Edmund L. Andrews, "Congress Votes New Communications Law," *The New York Times*, February 2, 1996, p. D6.

Glossary

addiction—A behavior that is harmful to one's self, but is hard to stop.

adultery—Sexual intercourse with someone when one partner is married to someone else.

appeals court—A higher court that reviews the verdict of a lower court.

bowdlerize—To censor or change language, as Bowdler did the works of Shakespeare.

censorship—Changing a work, or preventing production or distribution of it.

cheesecake—Pictures of women in provocative costumes.

comstockery—To behave in an aggressively prudish manner.

Constitution—The seven articles and twenty-two amendments that are the supreme law of the United States.

deprave—To lead into bad behavior; to corrupt.

Dial-A-Porn—Telephone numbers that can be called for obscene conversation at very high rates.

erotica—Material with sexually explicit content.

feminist—One who stands for equal rights for women.

flip book—Obscene drawings in sequence that seem to move when the pages are turned quickly.

hard-core—Explicit descriptions of sex acts or scenes of actual sex acts.

kiddy porn—Child pornography.

licentious—Ignoring sexual restraints.

obscenity—That which is offensive to decency.

perversion—Any act that deviates from the norm.

pornography—Writings, pictures, etc., intended to arouse sexual desire; obscene material.

prurient—Having lustful ideas or desires.

rape—Forcing a person to have sex against his or her will.

sensualist—One who overindulges in sensual pleasures.

sexologist—One who studies or treats sexual problems.

sexual revolution—The rebellion against strict morality in the 1960s that led to many people becoming more sexually active.

sexually explicit—Showing nudity or lustful acts.

smut—Pornography.

soft-core—Descriptions or scenes of sex acts that are not explicit.

stag films—Movies that were once illegal because they showed nudity and/or sex acts.

unconstitutional—Not in keeping with the laws set down in the United States Constitution and therefore not legal.

United States Supreme Court—The highest court in the United States; the court of last appeal; the final judge of what is legal under the Constitution, and what is not.

victim—One hurt by a crime.

X-rated—Having a rating of X due to explicit sexual material or activity.

Further Reading

Bode, Janet. *The Voices of Rape.* New York: Franklin Watts, 1990.

Brownmiller, Susan. *Against Our Will: Men, Women and Rape.* New York: Simon and Schuster, 1975.

Cline, Dr. Victor B., ed. *Where Do You Draw the Line? Explorations in Media Violence, Pornography & Censorship.* Provo, Utah: Brigham Young University Press, 1974.

De Grazia, Edward. *Girls Lean Back Everywhere: The Law of Obscenity and the Assault on Genius.* New York: Random House, 1992.

Forsyth, Dr. Elizabeth H., and Margaret O. Hyde. *The Violent Mind.* New York: Franklin Watts, 1991.

Heilbrun, Carolyn G. *The Education of a Woman: The Life of Gloria Steinem.* New York: The Dial Press, 1995.

Kendrick, Walter. *The Secret Museum: Pornography in Modern Culture.* New York: Viking, 1987.

Medved, Michael. *Hollywood vs. America.* New York: HarperCollins, 1992.

Newton, David E. *Teen Violence: Out of Control.* Springfield, N.J.: Enslow Publishers, Inc., 1995.

Strossen, Nadine. *Defending Pornography: Free Speech, Sex, and the Fight for Women's Rights.* New York: Scribner, 1995.

Swisher, Karin L., ed. *Teenage Sexuality: Opposing Viewpoints.* San Diego: Greenhaven Press, Inc., 1994.

Zeinert, Karen. *Free Speech: From Newspapers to Music Lyrics.* Springfield, N.J.: Enslow Publishers, Inc., 1995.

Index